CW00555200

CONTENTS

What is Erotic?

In *Road to Utopia* (1945), Dorothy Lamour says to Bob Hope, "It seems to me we've met before – perhaps in your dreams." "You wouldn't be seen in those kinds of places," is his answer. In dreams we can imagine a world of limitless sensual pleasure that is forbidden in our ordinary life of social constraints and religious restrictions. Here is another exchange from a movie: "Where I come from," says Pier Angeli, "nothing is evil. Everything that gives pleasure is good." Stewart Granger asks, "Where you do come from?" "Not far," she says. "Just ahead. Sodom and Gomorrah." (*Sodom and Gomorrah*, 1962) Erotic movies are a dream world where we live out the sinful, shameless and infinitely gratifying sexual fantasies that are off-limits in real life. According to psychoanalyst C. G. Jung, 'The cinema… makes it possible to experience without danger all the excitement, passion, and desirousness which must be repressed in a humanitarian ordering of life.'

Jean Harlow
Actress Jean Harlow reportedly dyed her pubic hair platinum blonde to match the hair on her head.

Movie stars are called sex gods and goddesses because they are larger than life, exhibiting a superabundant physicality on the screen, a riot of flesh and fantasy. The heaving breasts of Marilyn Monroe, the enfolding lips of Angelina Jolie, the tumid torso of Brad Pitt – these actors and actresses are the embodiments of our desire. They take us to heights of pleasure we mere mortals could never reach on our own. Some have said that the intensely erotic appeal of movie stars is dangerously seductive, leading us into a fantasy world of perfect, but false, fulfilment. "Most people don't have the energy for true passion, so they give up and go to the movies," says Jeanne Moreau, and Naim Kattan warns that, 'The photo of a film star leads, not to sensual joy with a living woman, but to another photo of another star, more daring and provocative than the first.' What real woman could ever live up to the ecstatic ideal of the screen sex goddess? Actress Rita Hayworth, after her sizzling striptease in *Gilda* (1946), was heard to complain that "Every man I've known has fallen in love with Gilda and wakened with me," while Cary Grant, one of the most magnetically handsome leading men in Hollywood, once ruefully admitted that he himself fell short of his image: "Everybody wants to be Cary Grant. Even I want to be Cary Grant."

But movie stars and sex scenes can be defended as stimulating additions to, not substitutes for, our real-life relationships, in the same way that erotic literature and art have helped us to envision new sensual possibilities. It is hard to imagine what witty sexual banter would be like if Mae West had never existed, as she herself

Audrey Dalton: "You must not be found in my room. If necessary, I will scream for help."
Bob Hope: "Oh, I don't need any help."

Casanova's Big Night (1954)

"A censor is a man who knows more than he thinks you ought to."

Laurence Peter

realized: "I didn't invent sex – I just rediscovered it, uncovered it, and gave it a couple of definitions that Mr. Webster never thought of." What if Clark Gable had never swept Vivien Leigh up the stairs in *Gone with the Wind* (1939), if Burt Lancaster and Deborah Kerr had never embraced on the beach in *From Here to Eternity* (1953), or if Marlon Brando and Maria Schneider had never straddled each other naked in *Last Tango in Paris* (1972)? The stars and scenes from these films are a vital part of our erotic image repertoire.

So, what exactly makes a movie erotic? Film scholar Molly Haskell once said that, "For a woman there is nothing more erotic than being understood." Why can't a man be both lustful and loving, cocky and committed? In *Roman Scandals* (1933), Eddie Cantor says to his beloved, "I can cook a little. I can take care of the children. If there are no children, I can take care of that." What scandalous effrontery to propose sex in the context of marriage and children! Such a scene enables women to envision an erotic ideal, combining the torrid and the tender in one man, as Lily Tomlin once said about actor John Travolta: "The sensitivity and the sexuality are very strong. It's as if he has every dichotomy – masculinity, femininity, refinement, crudity." Some sex goddesses offer a similar appeal to men, bringing together the naughty and the nice in one woman, moving both body and soul. Actress Nastassja Kinski "combines the innocent look of an angel with the guilty appeal of a sex kitten," says Terry Willows. A passionate union of equals is what is imagined in *Arabian Nights* (*Il fiore delle mille e una notte*, 1974). In one of this film's fanciful scenes, a sleeping young man and woman are tested to see who will fall for the other's greater beauty. The young man wakes, sees the woman, spreads her legs and enters her, then goes back to sleep. The young woman wakes, sees the man, rubs and mounts him, then goes back to sleep. The result of the test is that both sexes are beautiful: "they love each other equally."

Still from 'Fatima's Dance' (1893)
This is belly dancer Fatima in all her glory, before prudes superimposed a white fence over her lewd gyrations in what became the first film scene to be censored.

Equality, understanding, fidelity, commitment – for some people, these sanctioned virtues actually deaden the libido, and sexual excitement can come only from their opposite, vice. According to philosopher Georges Bataille, 'Eroticism always entails a breaking down of established patterns, [the taboos defined by] the regulated social order…The domain of eroticism is that of the transgression of these taboos…Vice can be thought of as the art of giving oneself the feeling of transgression." Since film is a visual medium, it should come as no surprise that one of erotic cinema's first transgressions is illicit looking, as a voyeuristic camera catches a nude woman bathing in *Le Tub* (*Après le Bal*, 1897). It is precisely because young women are thought of as modest, virginal, spiritual creatures that invading their privacy to spy on their naked flesh is so arousing. James Moore could be describing any one of a hundred T&A moments in films through the years, such as the salacious slow-motion shot of a high school girls' locker room in *Carrie* (1976), when he writes that: 'Movies with scenes set in women's showers inevitably portray them as brightly lit, open playrooms where nude women laugh, frolic, and snap each other with towels. Those not participating in high jinks are slowly and seductively soaping themselves under the shower spray.' This is the secret world of female desire that men would like to think they would find if they could see behind the ladies' prim and proper exterior.

Like voyeurism's guilty gaze, the illicit liaison known as adultery can make for a powerfully erotic scene. Adultery is everything marriage is not: novel, volatile, furtive, forbidden. In *Fatal Attraction* (1987), lovers Michael Douglas and Glenn Close invade the very sanctum of married life and domesticity when he drops his

Still from 'The May Irwin-John C. Rice Kiss' (1896)

Not exactly 'Last Tango in Paris' (1972), but this – the very first kiss on film – was thought to be scandalous at the time.

trousers and enters her as she is sitting on the kitchen sink. Rather than doing dishes, they are having hot sex, as she uses water from the kitchen tap to cool herself down during his thrusting. In *Pola X* (1999), Guillaume Depardieu leaves his wealthy and refined blonde fiancée for her opposite: a darkly sensual refugee woman (Katerina Golubeva). Their furtive tryst in an ill-lit room is shot to emphasize the graphic physicality of their "dirty" love, as he fingers her, she fellates him and finally he penetrates her to orgasm. Since she is his half-sister, incest can be added to infidelity as another taboo they transgress with their passion.

For some people, the erotic is what disrupts marriage as a stable union of equals, introducing the excitement of a sadomasochistic power imbalance. In *The Ages of Lulu* (*Las Edades de Lulú*, 1990), Oscar Ladoire binds, blindfolds and gags his wife Francesca Neri, then cuts open her panties so that he and her brother can have sex with her. Since she is kept in the dark, she only gradually realizes that a third man is involved and that he is her brother. Adultery, incest, a threesome, S&M – this scene explodes into eroticism by detonating multiple taboos. Such a scene allows married viewers to explore erotic extremes through on-screen fantasies that would destroy

ABOVE

Still from 'Häxan (Witchcraft Through the Ages)' (1922)

A witches' Sabbath in the forest reveals some sacrilegious nudity as the lecherous Devil (played by director Benjamin Christensen) reaches down to claim his bride. Häxan Films, the creators of 'The Blair Witch Project' (1999), took their name from this movie.

RIGHT

Publicity still for 'A Fool There Was' (1915)

Sexy vamp Theda Bara after she has sucked a man dry.

OPPOSITE

Still from 'The Queen of Sheba' (1921)

Betty Blythe is a vision of queenly enticement in her sheer pearl dress.

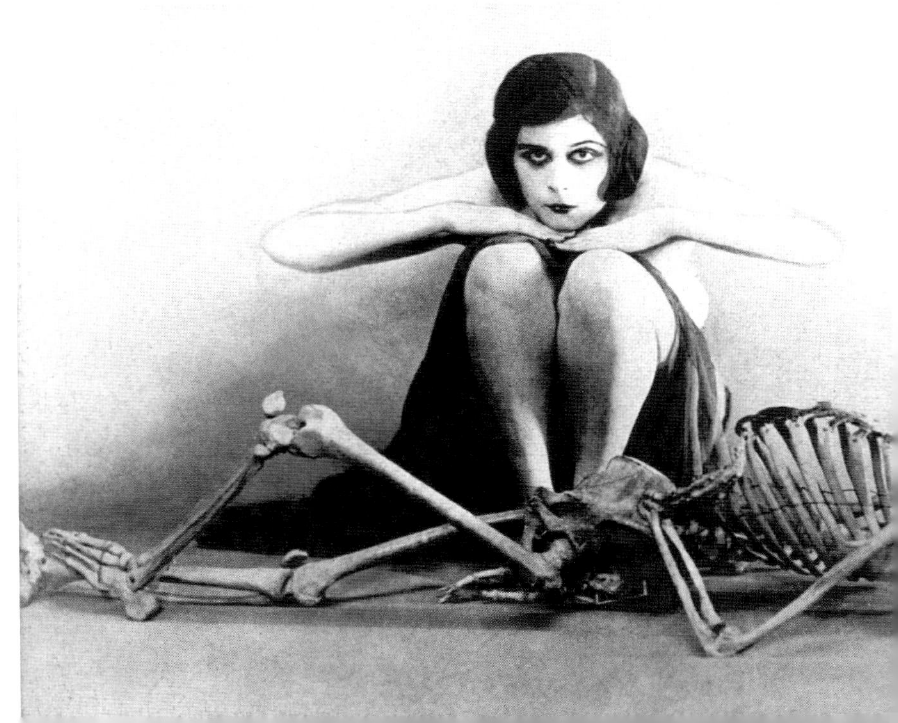

their relationship if acted out in real life. As psychiatrist Peter Dally writes, 'the man with strong sadistic fantasies cannot permit them to engulf the woman he idealizes; the woman's masochistic fantasies of rape and slavery fail to be kindled by her kind, considerate husband…Civilization obviously requires its members to suppress fantasies that are antisocial and sadistic. But much human unhappiness, dissatisfaction and destructive behaviour derive from the way people suppress harmless fantasies, out of ignorance and a sense of shame.'

The sexual charge of an S&M scene can also come from the thrill of social role reversal, where "normally" submissive females suddenly wield power, and dominant males are at their mercy, forced to experience the most exquisite pain. In *The Piano Teacher* (*La Pianiste*, 2001), music professor Isabelle Huppert masturbates male student Benoît Magimel in a campus restroom, but stops just as he is about to climax, refusing to relieve his blue balls and forbidding him to do so himself. As Susan Sontag points out, 'Human sexuality… belongs, at least potentially, among the extreme rather than the ordinary experiences of humanity. Tamed as it may be, sexuality remains one of the demonic forces in human consciousness – pushing us at intervals close to taboo and dangerous desires, which range from the impulse to commit sudden arbitrary violence upon another person to the voluptuous yearning for the extinction of one's consciousness, for death itself.' In *Videodrome* (1983),

ABOVE
Still from 'Blood and Sand' (1922)
Bullfighter Rudolph Valentino falls victim to a love bite from vamp Nita Naldi.

OPPOSITE
Still from 'The Sheik' (1921)
Rudolph Valentino makes passionate love to Agnes Ayres in the tent seduction scene. Valentino started a Latin lover craze in the 1920s, when men slicked their hair with Vaseline and kissed women's palms. Later, a condom would be named after him.

Still from 'Ben-Hur' (1925)
Bare-breasted nymphs strew flowers to celebrate the triumphant return of warriors Frank Currier and Ramon Novarro on horseback.

Publicity still for 'Ben-Hur' (1925)
This photo, with its slightly air-brushed pubic region, offers a tantalizing glimpse of Ramon Novarro, the Mexican-born hunk who competed with Rudolph Valentino as a 1920s sex symbol.

ABOVE

Still from 'Gold Diggers of 1933' (1933)

A scene from the 'Pettin' in the Park' number where the Peeping Tom camera looks up the girls' skirts.

LEFT

Still from 'Gold Diggers of 1933' (1933)

After getting soaked in a rainstorm, the girls run to change behind a screen, but its transparency only serves to call attention to their nudity.

OPPOSITE

Publicity still for 'Gold Diggers of 1933' (1933)

Chorus girl Ruby Keeler in a modestly showy moment.

RIGHT
Errol Flynn
The irresistible Errol Flynn once said, "A star doesn't have to pursue or seduce any woman. What he needs, more likely, is a chastity belt for self-protection." Here some attempt has been made to tone down his sexiness by having his nipples air-brushed out.

BELOW
Still from 'Cinema Paradiso' (1988)
Every time that two characters embrace on the screen, the village priest rings a bell to indicate that the kiss must be cut from the film.

masochist Deborah Harry intensifies the feeling of being penetrated by James Woods by having him burn her breasts with cigarettes and pierce her ears during their lovemaking. In *Viridiana* (1961), grieving widower Fernando Rey dresses his niece, a novice nun (Silvia Pinal), in his deceased wife's wedding gown, has her drugged and laid out on a bed, and then buries his head between her breasts – before stopping himself from going any further. Incest, sacrilege, rape and necrophilia – for some viewers, this scene is extremely erotic in that it breaks the strongest taboos.

Is it obscene? Yes, in the philosophical sense that transgression needs taboos to violate, standards of decency to defy, sins to commit. The prudes and moralists who want to censor and ban erotic films only fan the flames of lust with their outrage. The first film to be censored for sexual content, *Fatima's Dance* (1893), had two white horizontal bands placed over a belly dancer, but the bands only served to frame and focus attention on the woman's navel and gyrating belly, making the image even more inflammatory. Certain erotic scenes could be excused if they occurred within a biblical epic that showed the transgressors being punished, but the juxtaposition of pagan lust and Christian moralizing actually made the sex seem deliciously sinful. In *The Sign of the Cross* (1932), Christian maiden Elissa Landi is tempted when a decadent Roman (Joyzelle Joyner) does an undulating lesbian dance, and Landi is later tied naked to a post and threatened with rape by a gorilla. Mae

"We are paid to have dirty minds."

Censor John Trevelyan

Still from 'Ecstasy' (1933)
Hedy Lamarr floating in the nude and making this movie 'The Most Whispered About Picture in the World' – one that was confiscated, cut and banned in some countries.

West's racy one-liners in films such as *I'm No Angel* (1933) were denounced by the Catholic Legion of Decency, which said that her 'sportive wise-cracking tends to create tolerance if not acceptance of things essentially evil.' But the greater the outcry, the bigger the crowds that flocked to her films, prompting her to quip, "I believe in censorship. After all, I made a fortune out of it."

Despite the fact that sex sold even better when Blue-noses attacked it, Hollywood was threatened by looming church boycotts and government intervention, so in 1934 the movie industry began to enforce the Production Code. This Code was a form of self-censorship, a set of content restrictions that all film-makers had to abide by if they wanted to get a seal of approval and have their films shown in the major theatres. The Code stipulated that 'The sanctity of the institution of marriage and the home shall be upheld. No film shall infer that casual or promiscuous sex relationships are the accepted or common thing…Passion should be treated in such a manner as not to stimulate the baser emotions.' What this meant in practice was that 'when two people were in bed, they had to be either wed or dead,' as writer George S. Kaufman sardonically put it. Indeed, even husbands were expected to keep one foot on the floor when they kissed their wives in bed, and twin beds replaced doubles in many films. What this restriction also meant was that everything having to do with beds became erotically charged with a

"We have Viagra. Why should it be that you are allowed to be chemically aroused but not visually?"

Censor James Ferman

'Once in a millennium the motion picture screen erupts in such a staggering spectacle of animal passion and brute force that the audience is left drained and breathless… It puts eroticism back one million years, sexploitation films forward one thousand years.'

From the ad for *One Million AC/DC* (1969), script by Ed Wood, Jr.

ABOVE
Still from 'Tarzan and His Mate' (1934)
A naked Jane (Maureen O'Sullivan) – or rather, her body double – finds herself at the mercy of a crocodile's carnal appetite.

OPPOSITE
Publicity still for 'Tarzan and His Mate' (1934)
Animal sexuality is exuded by Jane (Maureen O'Sullivan) in two-piece jungle outfit as she clings to Tarzan (Johnny Weissmuller), who is wearing a loincloth and dagger.

barely repressed passion. This can be seen from censor Joseph Breen's objection to Greta Garbo's bedroom conduct in *Queen Christina* (1933), which seems quite tame by our current standards: 'Miss Garbo should be kept away from the bed entirely. The business of lying across the bed and fondling the pillow is, in my considered judgment, very offensive.'

The Code restrictions led to over 30 years of sexually suggestive imagery and double-entendre dialogue, and entire careers were made from a blending of tease and tut-tut, such as that of "professional virgin" Doris Day. In movies like *Pillow Talk* (1959) with Rock Hudson, she is all talk and no action, all hugs and no kisses. One critic said about Day and Hudson, 'When these two magnificent objects go into a clinch, aglow from the sunlamp, agleam with hair lacquer, they look less like creatures of flesh than a couple of Cadillacs parked in a suggestive position.' Film reviewer John Simon saw Doris Day's unsullied virginity as a sign of cinema's arrested development: 'The only real talent Miss Day possesses is that of being absolutely sanitary, her form unsmudged by the slightest evidence of femininity…Until this spun-sugar zombie melts from our screen there is little chance of the American film's coming of age.'

A brazen challenge to the Production Code's reign of censorship was made by *The Moon is Blue* (1953), a comedy that dared to use words like "virgin", "seduce" and "mistress", and one whose heroine was a little too curious: "Don't you think it's better for a girl to be preoccupied with sex than occupied?" Censor Joseph Breen had condemned the film for its 'unacceptably light attitude toward seduction, illicit sex, chastity and virginity', but despite his refusal to grant the film a seal of approval, the studio released it anyway to some theatres willing to defy the Code. Audiences were eager to see what had so scandalized the censor, and they made the movie a hit. The next 15 years saw a gradual loosening of the Code's restrictions as more movies pushed the erotic envelope and, due to increasingly liberal sexual attitudes, eventually were given Code approval. Landmarks in the history of erotic cinema include the following as among the first films to break the Code's ban on lesbianism (*The Children's Hour*, 1961), miscegenation (*Island in the Sun*, 1957), adultery (*The Apartment*, 1960), prostitution (*Butterfield 8*, 1960), and paedophilia (*Lolita*, 1962). Admittedly, these films were still fairly tame in their treatment of risqué subjects, not really showing much at all, but a few films were more flagrant in what they revealed: *Splendor in the Grass* (1961) featured a French kiss; *The Pawnbroker* (1965) uncovered a woman's bare breasts; and *Psycho* (1960) showed a woman being stabbed in the shower (implied rape).

In 1968, the Code with its censorious restrictions was finally replaced by a ratings system designed to be merely advisory, describing rather than proscribing the content of films. Audiences no longer had to make do with rumours about the things censors had kept them from seeing. Now these things could be shown, and the ratings would help by guiding viewers toward the films with the naughtiest bits. Female nudity and breast-fondling could be found in an R-rated film, but for erections and fellatio – along with cunnilingus and penetration – audiences would have to seek out an X. And X-rated films like *Deep Throat* (1972) were suddenly playing in mainstream theatres, drawing excited crowds bursting with pent-up demand after years of repression.

But sexual freedom never lasts for long. In its 1973 *Miller v. California* decision, the US Supreme Court gave power to local states and regions to ban whatever films they considered to be obscene according to their own 'community standards'. The

Still from 'Romance' (1999)
Paulo (played by porn star Rocco Siffredi) works on giving Marie (Caroline Ducey) some of the hard loving she cannot get from her boyfriend, whose interest in her is flagging.

"They are in love, and in this scene they make love with joy, sincerity, and the passion which this act deserves. There is no social system that forbids two healthy young lovers from enjoying the pleasure that nature has bestowed. Luckily, nobody can take that away from them – not even Jack Valenti and his whole Motion Picture Association of America."

Director Pedro Almodóvar on the love scene in *Tie Me Up! Tie Me Down!* (1990)

threat of local prosecution on obscenity charges effectively ended the showing of X-rated films in mainstream theatres, making it financially disastrous for the major studios to produce them. Moreover, in the 1980s, national video chains such as Blockbuster refused to stock X-rated films. A clever attempt was made to sneak erotic films back into theatres and video stores by creating a new rating, NC-17, which was designed to distinguish sexually daring films of artistic value from mere smut. However, conservative pressure groups shamed people into staying away from theatrical screenings of NC-17 films and, once again, Blockbuster Video refused to carry them in America.

Nevertheless, as in the days of the Production Code, all this preaching and prohibition has stimulated even greater interest in films deemed forbidden fruit. NC-17 movies such as *Henry & June* (1990) and *Showgirls* (1995) that did poor box office in public venues have had great success on videotape and DVD, which people can watch in the privacy of their own homes and rent from mail-order companies like Netflix. Unrated and 'director's cut' versions of R-rated movies, with the censored bits added back in, are wildly popular. And recently, a group of unrated art and independent films, including *L'Humanité* (1999), *Baise-Moi* (2000), *The Brown Bunny* (2003), and *9 Songs* (2004), has created a *succès de scandale* by including hardcore scenes of real sex within mainstream movies.

Perhaps the most notorious film in this group is director Catherine Breillat's *Romance* (1999), a movie as serious in its exploration of eroticism as it is explicit in what it shows. Teacher Marie (Caroline Ducey) is emotionally involved with her

boyfriend Paul (Sagamore Stévenin), but when she cannot raise his flagging interest in her by fellating him, she picks up a stud named Paolo (Rocco Siffredi), slips a condom over his erection, and enjoys vigorous rear-entry sex. Marie's life is split, but she wants to find one man who can give her both emotional and physical fulfilment. She goes home with her boss (François Berléand), whose manner is exceptionally kind and considerate even as he binds and gags her, pushes her dress up and her panties down, and pulls a rope tight between her legs, provoking her to moan. Is Marie discovering her potential for masochistic pleasure, or does she want to be punished because she feels that her strong desire for sex is sinful in a woman? The film goes on to present scenes of masturbation, cunnilingus and penetration – not as mere porn, but as a passionate enquiry into the complexities of sex.

Still from 'Romance' (1999)
Marie claims the right to sexual fulfilment. This image appeared on the poster for the film with a red X over her sex, indicating patriarchy's denial of female desire. When the film was first released in France, it was given an X rating, which banned it from mainstream theatres.

"The taboos, prohibitions and shame that surround women's sexuality are necessary because desire comes from taboos. But at the same time… they have to be transgressed. If they cannot be transgressed they turn into morality and censorship, which end up harming women."

Director Catherine Breillat

Kissing / Romance

Erotic film history gets off to a somewhat shaky start when John C. Rice strokes his handlebar moustache and then awkwardly bumps noses with matronly May Irwin as they lock lips in *The Kiss* (1896). But this middle-aged smooch was inflammatory because it appeared on the big screen, and so film's first erotic moment also became the first to provoke calls for censorship. As Chicago publisher Harold S. Stone wrote, 'the spectacle of their prolonged pasturing on each other's lips was hard to bear when only life size. Magnified to Gargantuan proportions… it is absolutely disgusting. Such things call for police interference.'

One leading man known for his sensational kisses was Clark Gable. A female fan once described Gable as "thrilling because no girl would feel safe with him for a minute". In *Hold Your Man* (1933), Gable gives Jean Harlow a kiss to remember. As Adrianne Blue describes it in her book *On Kissing*, 'Gable was a master, crushing his leading lady to him so that her head or his obscured their lips, creating an illusion of passion without actually showing the kiss…In mid-kiss, he pulls her body into his, hard. One gets the sense of forceful joining from the violence of the arm, not the lips. He is the kisser, she the kissed.' In *Gone with the Wind* (1939), Gable tells Vivien Leigh, "You should be kissed, and often, and by someone who knows how." When she says that she'll faint from his kisses, his reply is, "I want you to faint. This is what you were meant for." Even Marilyn Monroe, who appeared with Gable in *The Misfits* (1961), was heard to comment, "Can you imagine what being kissed by him meant to me?"

Some of the most memorable kissing scenes are also accompanied by sexy pillow talk, which is not surprising given that both are forms of oral foreplay. In *Cactus Flower* (1969), when Walter Matthau tells Ingrid Bergman that "I think I'm going to kiss you," her reply – "When will you know for sure?" – is sweetly encouraging, and Lauren Bacall tries to give Humphrey Bogart some extra incentive when she tells him during a kiss that "It's even better when you help" (*To Have and Have Not*, 1944). What Deborah Kerr says to Burt Lancaster in their passionate beach scene is something that every man wants to hear: "I never knew it could be like this. Nobody ever kissed me the way you do." (*From Here to Eternity*, 1953) At the opposite extreme, when vamp Theda Bara tells a wayward husband, "Kiss me, my fool," in *A Fool There Was* (1914), she is asserting her seductive power over him to keep him from returning to his wife. (The line became a catchphrase repeated by

ABOVE
Still from 'Gone with the Wind' (1939)
Clark Gable carries a struggling Vivien Leigh upstairs to a bedroom where he will overcome her resistance.

OPPOSITE
Still from 'Gone with the Wind' (1939)
A kiss from commanding Rhett Butler (Clark Gable) causes Scarlett O'Hara (Vivien Leigh) to swoon. Actress Ursula Thiess once said that "Clark Gable made you feel twice the woman you thought you were."

"Ernst Lubitsch could do more with a closed door than most of today's directors can do with an open fly."

Director Billy Wilder

RIGHT
Still from 'Brief Encounter' (1945)
Handsome doctor Trevor Howard removes a piece of grit from Celia Johnson's eye and she sees that he is the man she loves.

BELOW
On the set of 'Brief Encounter' (1945)
Filming the romantic row on the lake. As Hugh Grant says, "Whatever happened to the days when sex was Celia Johnson and Rachmaninoff on the piano?"

Still from 'Casablanca' (1942)
The famous non-kissing scene where Humphrey Bogart and Ingrid Bergman say farewell. According to Bogart, "I did nothing in 'Casablanca' that I hadn't done in twenty movies before that and suddenly they discover I'm sexy. Any time that Ingrid Bergman looks at a man, he has sex appeal."

women all over America, who commanded their men to "Kiss me, you fool.")

From a prude's perspective, kissing first began to get out of control early in film history. Greta Garbo's blatantly open-mouthed kisses with John Gilbert in *Flesh and the Devil* (1927) made no secret of the fact that she was actually falling in love with her co-star at the time, while in *The Sea Beast* (1925) four takes of the same kiss were edited together to extend John Barrymore's lip-lock with Dolores Costello, after which she was said to have fainted on the set. Barrymore was at it again in *Don Juan* (1926), emphasizing quantity this time over length: he kisses Mary Astor and Estelle Taylor 127 times, which is still the record for the most in a single film. It is no wonder that the censors who wrote the 1930 Production Code made a point of prohibiting 'lustful', 'prolonged' or 'excessive' kissing, along with 'evidently lustful embraces'. That didn't stop Regis Toomey and Jane Wyman from kissing for three minutes and five seconds in *You're in the Army Now* (1940), but this was okay in a comedy. Alfred Hitchcock had a harder time getting away with it in a romantic thriller like *Notorious* (1946), but he got around the restriction that no on-screen kiss should last longer than three seconds by having Cary Grant and Ingrid Bergman kiss, then nibble, kiss again, then caress, kiss, then answer the phone – and so on in a marathon make-out session that is actually sexier than it would have been if they had not kept on bringing their lips together again and again.

Some of the most romantic kisses involve an element of mystery. In *The Scarlet Empress* (1934), Marlene Dietrich holds a gauze veil over her face before allowing John Lodge to kiss her, while Grace Kelly appears to move in soft-focus slow motion when she bends down to kiss James Stewart as he is waking up in *Rear Window* (1954). A subtle, symbolic kiss occurs in *Now, Voyager* (1942) when Paul Henreid lights up two cigarettes in his mouth and then hands one to Bette Davis. (After appearing in this scene, the actor couldn't go anywhere without being accosted by women begging him to "light me".) More comically, Dustin Hoffman

'There is evidence in more than one quarter that the cinema taught girls the trick of closing their eyes when kissed, which one had always supposed to be a natural instinct of women. It encouraged them to kick up one heel (or even two heels) when embraced. It also taught them how and when to slap.'

E.S. Turner, ***A History of Courting***

ABOVE
Still from 'The 39 Steps' (1935)
Because they are handcuffed together, Madeleine Carroll has no choice but to let Robert Donat share in some intimate moments, such as slipping off her stocking.

RIGHT
Still from 'The Age of Innocence' (1993)
Michelle Pfeiffer burns at the mere touch of Daniel Day-Lewis as they are drawn together in spite of high society's disapproval.

OPPOSITE
Still from 'Red Dust' (1932)
The harlot Jean Harlow seduces Clark Gable. The brazenly bra-less Harlow was known for such roles and would ask her agent, "What kinda whore am I this time?"

kisses Anne Bancroft right after she takes a drag on her cigarette, causing her to hold the smoke until their lips part in *The Graduate* (1967). The idea that a kissing couple can make sparks fly is seen in *To Catch a Thief* (1955) when the meeting of lips between Grace Kelly and Cary Grant causes fireworks to erupt in the sky behind them, while in *Touch of Evil* (1958) the explosive potential of an interracial embrace is realized when the kiss between Charlton Heston (playing a Mexican) and Janet Leigh seems to detonate a car bomb. Two films present homages to cinematic osculation: *Billy's Hollywood Screen Kiss* (1998) has Sean Hayes shooting a photo series in which he re-creates great screen kisses from Hollywood's Golden Age, and *Cinema Paradiso* (1988) ends with a montage of all the spliced-together kissing scenes that have been cut from movies which a local town priest has censored over the years.

"The mind can also be an erogenous zone."

Raquel Welch

Although outlawing kisses may be going too far, there are some who believe that censorship actually helped rather than hurt film eroticism by requiring movies to be sexily suggestive rather than anatomically in-your-face. As Mae West once pointed out, "Let's face it, the sex organs ain't got no personality." Plus, there is such a thing as being over-exposed. In *A League of Their Own* (1992), Madonna asks, "What if, at a key moment in the game, my uniform bursts open and – oops! – my bosoms come flying out? That might draw a crowd, right?" Rosie O'Donnell replies, "You think there are men in this country who ain't seen your bosoms?" There is a greater erotic charge in *Flashdance* (1983) when Jennifer Beals removes her black bra from under her sweatshirt while sitting in front of a guy than there would be if she had exposed her breasts to him. When it comes to sex on screen, less can be more. Bette Davis once commented that "I certainly agree with all those who find more sex appeal in Barbara Stanwyck and her ankle bracelet in *Double Indemnity* [1944] than in all these naked bodies rolling around on the screen today." Sophia Loren believed that "Sex appeal is 50% what you've got and 50% what people think you've got," while Hedy Lamarr said, "If you use your imagination, you can look at any actress and see her nude. I hope to make you use your imagination."

ABOVE
Still from 'Before Sunrise' (1995)
Ethan Hawke and Julie Delpy spend the night exploring each other – through conversation.

OPPOSITE
Still from 'The Thomas Crown Affair' (1968)
Faye Dunaway is looking suggestively at Steve McQueen as she fingers the pieces in this game of chess as foreplay.

A touch can be all it takes to send sensual ripples through a scene. When Trevor Howard removes a speck of grit from Celia Johnson's eye in *Brief Encounter* (1945), it is more moving than if he had thrown his arms around her. Similarly, in *Pillow Talk* (1959) when Doris Day and Rock Hudson stretch out in separate bathtubs and their bare feet are made to touch through the magic of split-screen, an erotic current seems to flow between them, as it does when Sophia Loren slides casually over Marcello Mastroianni's lap as they change places in the backseat of her Rolls Royce in *Yesterday, Today, and Tomorrow* (*Ieri, oggi, domani*, 1963). More recently, a bare-chested Patrick Swayze sits behind Demi Moore as their hands entwine in the wet clay on the potter's wheel in *Ghost* (1990).

For some viewers, the sexiest scenes are those that combine powerful longing and lack of fulfilment. Director Elia Kazan has said, "What I find erotic is amorous pursuit. To show the act itself is not erotic. What is erotic is 'Will he or won't he get her?' And 'Will she or won't she get him?' The arousal of desire is erotic, as well as the presence of desire before it is satisfied." In *Last Year at Marienbad* (*L'Année dernière à Marienbad*, 1961), Giorgio Albertazzi is caught in an endless loop in which he approaches but never quite attains his beloved Delphine Seyrig before having to start all over again: "And one more time, I advanced along these same hallways, walking for days, for months, for years, to meet you." Balthazar Getty spends most of *Lost Highway* (1997) pursuing Patricia Arquette, but when he seems closest to

ABOVE

Still from 'Sunrise' (1927)

Farmer George O'Brien is led astray by a wicked city woman who tries to get him to drown his wife. When his love is renewed for good wife Janet Gaynor, their kiss literally stops traffic.

RIGHT

Still from 'A Place in the Sun' (1951)

Elizabeth Taylor and Montgomery Clift share a kiss. "Montgomery Clift was the most sensitive man I've ever known. If somebody kicked a dog a mile away he'd feel it," said director Edward Dmytryk.

ABOVE

Still from 'From Here to Eternity' (1953)

It is impossible to imagine film history without Burt Lancaster and Deborah Kerr's passionate embrace on the beach, but having their kiss occur here was actually a last-minute inspiration by director Fred Zinnemann.

LEFT

Still from 'Rear Window' (1954)

Grace Kelly gives James Stewart a kiss and asks how his "leg" is doing. (His leg is in a cast due to an accident.)

Still from 'Ghost' (1990)
Demi Moore's lover, Patrick Swayze, is dead, but she feels his palpable presence at the potter's wheel.

Still from 'Love Story' (1970)
Impending death adds poignancy to the romance between Ali MacGraw and Ryan O'Neal, who muses at the end, "What can you say about a 25-year-old girl who died? That she was beautiful and brilliant? That she loved Mozart and Bach, the Beatles and me?"

realizing his white-hot passion, when they are finally naked together in the desert sand lit up by bright car headlights, she puts her mouth to his ear and whispers, "You'll never have me." James Stewart believes that the beloved he lost has come back to him in the person of Kim Novak, and the camera does an ecstatic 360-degree swirl around him as he kisses and embraces her in *Vertigo* (1958), but by the end of the film his arms will be holding only air as his reach cannot stop her from falling to her death. And the most famous *non*-kissing scene occurs at the end of *Casablanca* (1942), where Humphrey Bogart and Ingrid Bergman put patriotism before passion as they sacrifice their love for each other in a farewell scene filled with repressed desire.

Judy Holliday: "What are you doing?"
William Holden: "Well, if you don't know, I must be doing it wrong."

Born Yesterday **(1950)**

Stills from 'Titanic' (1997)
Top: Trusting Leonardo DiCaprio to hold her, Kate Winslet learns how to fly.
Above: Kate Winslet poses for Leonardo DiCaprio: "I want you to draw me like one of your French girls, wearing this [necklace] – wearing only this."

Humphrey Bogart: "Speaking of horses, you've got a touch of class, but I don't know how far you can go."
Lauren Bacall: "A lot depends on who's in the saddle."

The Big Sleep **(1946)**

Nudity / Sex Goddess / Femme Fatale / Hunk

Among the first films to cause a sensation due to full-frontal female nudity was *Ecstasy* (*Extase*, 1933) in which star Hedwig Kiesler (later known as Hedy Lamarr) is glimpsed running naked through the trees and bathing in a river. This Czech film was confiscated by US Customs and burned as obscene, and Lamarr's husband later tried to buy and destroy all prints of the film to keep the world from seeing his wife nude. Some believe that it was not so much the sight of Lamarr naked in nature that upset the censors as the naked expression of ecstasy on her face as she orgasms during intercourse in one of the film's other scenes. A similar point about female exposure was made more recently with *The Cooler* (2003). While the MPAA ratings board claimed to object to a glimpse of Maria Bello's pubic hair that can be seen while William H. Macy gives her cunnilingus, Bello believes that "the reason the scene had to get cut was not about the pubic hair", but about the close-up of her "face having an orgasm – a real one, a complicated one – a woman deriving pleasure".

There are cases where veiled or partial nudity can be more exciting than open display. In *A Free Soul* (1931), Norma Shearer wears a transparent, form-fitting gown of white satin which reveals that she doesn't have a stitch on underneath. As co-star Clark Gable was heard to comment, "Damn, the dame doesn't wear any underwear in her scenes. Is she doing that in the interests of realism or what?" And gossip columnist Cal York wrote about Shearer that 'when she is having her clothes designed for picture purposes, she insists that they show as much of her anatomy as the law and [censor] Will Hays allow.' Jean Harlow was another star who shocked viewers when she slipped into something more comfortable, as in *China Seas* (1935) where she is wrapped in a wet, see-through silk negligee. Harlow went bra-less under her clothes and she was known to ice her nipples to keep them perky, thus provoking a shift in erotic focus from the legs of 1920s' flappers to female breasts in the 1930s. In *Red Dust* (1932), Harlow alarmed the censors in a scene where Clark Gable can see her naked breasts as she bathes in a rain barrel. *We* cannot see them, but apparently during filming, Harlow stood up in the bath and flashed them, saying "Something for the boys in the lab!"

Harlow and Shearer were among the screen's early sex goddesses, mere figures of light and shadow but perceived as full-bodied incarnations of sensuality. As film historian Richard Griffith writes, 'To sit in the dark and behold a beauty that

Still from 'La dolce vita' (1960)
Anita Ekberg came to prominence when she cavorted in the waters of Rome's Trevi Fountain, representing a pure uninhibited sexuality.

Gene Kelly: "That's quite a dress you almost have on. What holds it up?"
Nina Foch: "Modesty."

An American in Paris **(1951)**

embodies all the dreams of men since time began is something new under the sun, and wonderful. If the movie camera needed justification, perhaps this is it.' No screen goddess was more elusive and alluring than Greta Garbo. Joan Crawford once commented that "One almost feels grateful to Garbo for keeping herself so resolutely to herself, for leaving us a little mystery," while François Mauriac said of Garbo: "This being, at one and the same time real and inaccessible, rouses all desire." Ramon Novarro is so drawn to Garbo in *Mata Hari* (1932) that he follows her bidding and blows out the candle of a holy Madonna's lamp to worship at Garbo's sensual shrine, and in *Flesh and the Devil* (1927) Garbo herself kneels at an altar and turns the communion chalice around to drink from the spot that her lover's mouth has just touched. As Mick LaSalle writes in *Complicated Women*, 'Garbo is literally a sex goddess, a saint of sex, assuring us that there are moments of physical ecstasy so profound that they take on a spiritual dimension.'

If goddess Garbo seduces by veiling sex as a sacred mystery, Jane Russell's bountiful charms are much more in-your-face. The metallic uplift bra that Howard Hughes engineered especially for Russell to wear in *The Outlaw* (1943) may have worked too well in that it brought her talents to the attention of censor Joseph Breen, who complained that 'the girl's breasts, which are quite large and prominent, are shockingly emphasized and in almost every instance are very substantially uncovered'. When Breen demanded cuts so that we would see less of Russell, Hughes fought back by measuring the busts on other sex goddesses in still photos from their films and then arguing that Russell actually showed *proportionately* less cleavage on screen than they did. Hughes finally released the film three years later without a censor's seal of approval and it proved to be a huge success – except in places where it was banned as obscene, such as the state of Maryland where a judge wrote that 'Russell's breasts hang over the picture like a summer thunderstorm spread out over a landscape.'

While an earth-mother goddess like Russell is prodigiously giving, a vamp like Marlene Dietrich sucks a man dry. In *The Blue Angel* (*Der Blaue Engel*, 1930), Dietrich ensnares men with a nightclub act in which she leans backward while seated on a barrel, using her arms to lift up one stockinged leg while seductively tilting her head. Professor Emil Jannings is in her thrall, even kneeling before her in her dressing room to slip black stockings onto her legs when she commands him to do so. Jean Cocteau once said to Marlene Dietrich that "Your name begins with a caress and ends with the crack of a whip," and Ernest Hemingway confessed, "I know that every time I've seen Marlene Dietrich, it has done something to my heart."

Like moths to a flame, men are drawn to the femme fatale – a point that Ann Sheridan makes in a comic line from *Take Me to Town* (1953): "I'm a flaming redhead. If you play with fire, you'll get burned." The femme fatale promises to give a man a good time, but it may be the last time – *la petite mort* made literal, as in *Invasion of the Bee Girls* (1973) where the men die happy "coming and going at the same time" as one envious but frightened friend says. 'The image of the vamp embodies two fantasies,' writes Mick LaSalle. 'The paranoid fantasy is that sex can kill you. The romantic fantasy is that it just might be worth it.'

Vamp Theda Bara as *Cleopatra* (1917) wears a gown with spidery embroidery over her pubis, while Monica Vitti as *Modesty Blaise* (1966) has a scorpion tattoo on her thigh. Bikini-clad Ursula Andress in *Dr. No* (1962) rises from the sea like Botticelli's Venus – except that she has a knife tied to her waist. Ballerina Daryl

ABOVE
Still from 'Bitter Rice' (1949)
Earthy, full-figured Silvana Mangano (seen here from behind) became a sex symbol of Italian neorealism.

OPPOSITE
Still from 'Sans lendemain' (1939)
1930s French sex symbol Edwige Feuillère gives a provocative performance at a nightclub known as The Siren.

Femmes Fatales

Left: 'Mata Hari' (1932) Greta Garbo as the dangerously seductive courtesan and spy. Alistair Cooke once said about Garbo that "She gave you the feeling that if your imagination has to sin, it can at least congratulate itself on its impeccable taste."

Bottom Left: 'Pandora's Box' (1929) A son (Francis Lederer) cradles his dying father (Fritz Kortner) after he has been shot by Lulu (Louise Brooks), the woman they both desire.

Below: 'Lust for a Vampire' (1971) Lesbian vampire Yutte Stensgaard satisfies her bloodlust.

Opposite Top: 'The Blue Angel' (1930) As nightclub singer Lola, Marlene Dietrich tempts men with her seeming accessibility, then tortures them by withholding herself. Dietrich made stockings popular as an erotic accessory.

Opposite Bottom Left: 'From Dusk Till Dawn' (1996) Vamp(ire) Santanico Pandemonium, played by Salma Hayek, has fangs just like her snake.

Opposite Bottom Right: 'Bedazzled' (2000) Elizabeth Hurley as the Devil in a flaming red bikini enjoys having a snake slither around her body.

ABOVE

Publicity still for 'The Outlaw' (1943)

A red-hot image of Jane Russell ready for a roll in the hay, with one shoulder bared, a slit skirt and a gun held against her thigh.

RIGHT

Mae West

Mae West's measurements (36-26-36) were published and celebrated. As she herself pointed out, "It isn't what I do, but how I do it. It isn't what I say, but how I say it. And how I look when I do it and say it."

OPPOSITE

Publicity still for 'Duel in the Sun' (1946)

Playing fiery half-breed Pearl Chavez, Jennifer Jones seems to have a handle on what she wants in a movie that was nicknamed 'Lust in the Dust.'

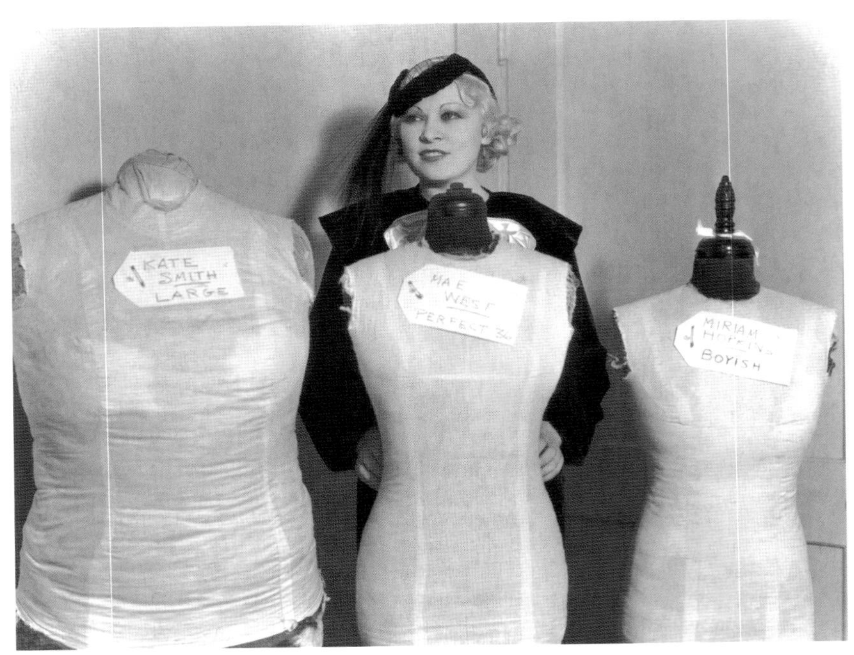

OPPOSITE
On the Set of 'Suddenly, Last Summer' (1959)
Elizabeth Taylor once said, "I have a woman's body and a child's emotions." In the film, Taylor's beautiful body is so irresistible that her male cousin uses it to lure young men to him.

BELOW
Publicity Still for 'Salome' (1953)
Salome (Rita Hayworth) does her seductive dance of the seven veils for her lover Claudius (Stewart Granger). Hayworth once said, "After all, a girl is – well, a girl. It's nice to be told you're successful at it."

"When you get a sex story in biblical garb, you can open your own mint."

Producer Darryl Zanuck

Hannah is sweetly seductive until she puts the squeeze on Harrison Ford's head between her thighs in *Blade Runner* (1982). Chesty Morgan uses her 73-inch breasts as *Deadly Weapons* (1973) to suffocate men, while buxom Ursula Andress fires at men with her double-barrelled brassiere in *The 10th Victim* (*La decima vittima*, 1965). And vampire Béatrice Dalle kisses men with her tumid lips and slakes her bloodlust, causing *Trouble Every Day* (2001).

There were of course seductively dangerous men – *hommes fataux* to counter the femmes. As *The Sheik* (1921), Rudolph Valentino kidnaps Agnes Ayres and carries her off to his tent, where he then smooth-talks her into sex. When she asks, "Why have you brought me here?" his answer is "Are you not woman enough to know?" Valentino exuded animal passion but was also a suave wooer. H.L. Mencken described him as 'catnip to women'. While Valentino was exotically alluring, Clark Gable's appeal was more rough and all-American. Biographer René Jordan writes that 'the screen Gable insinuated he had a power to give orgasms, even to a generation of women who still were not too sure whether they were supposed to have them.' After Gable opened his shirt to reveal a hairy bare chest in *It Happened One Night* (1934), sales in men's undershirts took a 40% drop. The sight of William Holden's matted torso was considered so incendiary that he had to shave his chest before it could appear in the scene where Rosalind Russell rips open his shirt in *Picnic* (1956). And Marlon Brando conveys a savage sexuality in his wet, torn T-shirt as he howls for his wife Stella in *A Streetcar Named Desire* (1951).

As for male nudity below the waist, it is less commonly seen than its female counterpart, perhaps because, as screenwriter Paul Rudnick notes, 'Male sexual equipment is judged a little more harshly at times, and more visibly. I think men see exposing themselves both as a form of powerlessness and as a global reckoning.' For the nude wrestling scene in *Women in Love* (1969) – the first commercial film to bare male genitals – Oliver Reed is said to have given himself some manual assistance after sizing up the competition presented by Alan Bates. And perhaps Javier Bardem and Tomás Penco draw courage from the macho context for their ballsy nude bullfighting scene in *Jamón, jamón* (1992).

"There aren't any hard women, only soft men."

Raquel Welch

ABOVE

Still from 'Barb Wire' (1996)

Buxom Pamela Anderson as a shoot-'em-up comic-book heroine shows that she really means it when she says, "Don't call me babe."

OPPOSITE

On the Set of 'Dr No' (1962)

A man on the film crew helpfully douses Ursula Andress with water for her beach scene as the beautiful but deadly Honey Ryder in this James Bond film.

ABOVE

Publicity still for 'One Million Years B.C.' (1966)

Raquel Welch in an animal-skin bikini invites us to 'discover a savage world whose only law was lust', as the ad for the film said.

OPPOSITE

Publicity still for '10' (1979)

Bo Derek as the ideal woman – a perfect "10". Derek once said, "I guess a film in which I didn't end up in bed, in the sea or in a hot tub would have the same appeal as a Clint Eastwood movie in which nobody got shot."

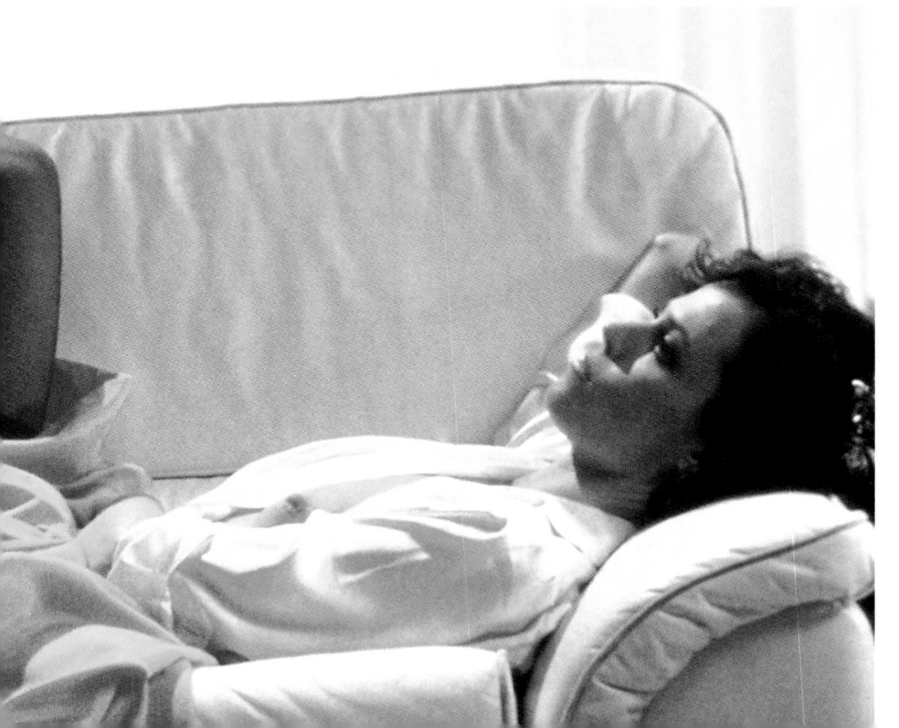

ABOVE
Still from 'Crimes of Passion' (1984)
Policeman John Laughlin submits to being handcuffed to a bed by prostitute Kathleen Turner and then sodomized with his own nightstick.

LEFT
Still from 'Half Moon Street' (1986)
Think-tank researcher Sigourney Weaver delves into the possibility of moonlighting as a high-priced call girl.

OPPOSITE
Still from 'The 10th Victim' (1965)
Ursula Andress as a futuristic assassin with a bra that shoots bullets.

'Extensive tour
Of D. Lamour,
Nearly all
Of Jon Hall.
Sudden panic,
Cause volcanic,
And a torso
Or so.'

Film reviewer C.A. Lejeune on *The Hurricane* (1937)

Hunks

Above: 'Risky Business' (1983) Horny teenager Tom Cruise dreams of sex and decides to make it happen by turning his parents' home into a whorehouse while they're away on vacation.

Top Right: 'A Streetcar Named Desire' (1951) Southern belle Blanche DuBois (Vivien Leigh) is up against the raw masculinity of Stanley Kowalski (Marlon Brando), who says, "You think I'm gonna interfere with you? Maybe you wouldn't be bad to interfere with."

Right: 'American Gigolo' (1980) This film made Richard Gere famous as a male escort who looks good in – and out of – his Armani suit. Gere was one of the first male stars not to shy away from doing full-frontal nudity.

Opposite: 'Barbarella' (1968) Jane Fonda is interested in the gun near the thigh of angel John Phillip Law, but he says, "An angel does not make love; an angel IS love."

Still from 'Betty Blue' (1986)
With her warm flesh tones and sensual lips, Betty (Béatrice Dalle) is the passionate embodiment of hope for the hero of this film.

Both male and female nudity are startlingly apparent from the very first frames of Jean-Jacques Beineix's *Betty Blue* (*37°2 le matin*, 1986), which begins with a lengthy shot of a man thrusting passionately on top of a woman. She reaches down to feel him going in and out of her, and then bites his shoulder when they both climax. *Betty Blue* is noteworthy for giving its lead actor and actress equal time when it comes to nudity, including full-frontal. The film is also fascinating in its presentation of an unusually complex sex goddess. With her bobbed dark hair, bee-stung lips, prominent front teeth, tattooed shoulder, and slight pot-belly, Béatrice Dalle plays Betty, a woman of unabashed sensuality who throws herself almost nymphomaniacally at her lover Zorg (Jean-Hugues Anglade). In one scene, she kisses his male member; in another, she spreads her legs and pulls his head down to her sex; and in a third, she straddles him in front of a fireplace and rides him to

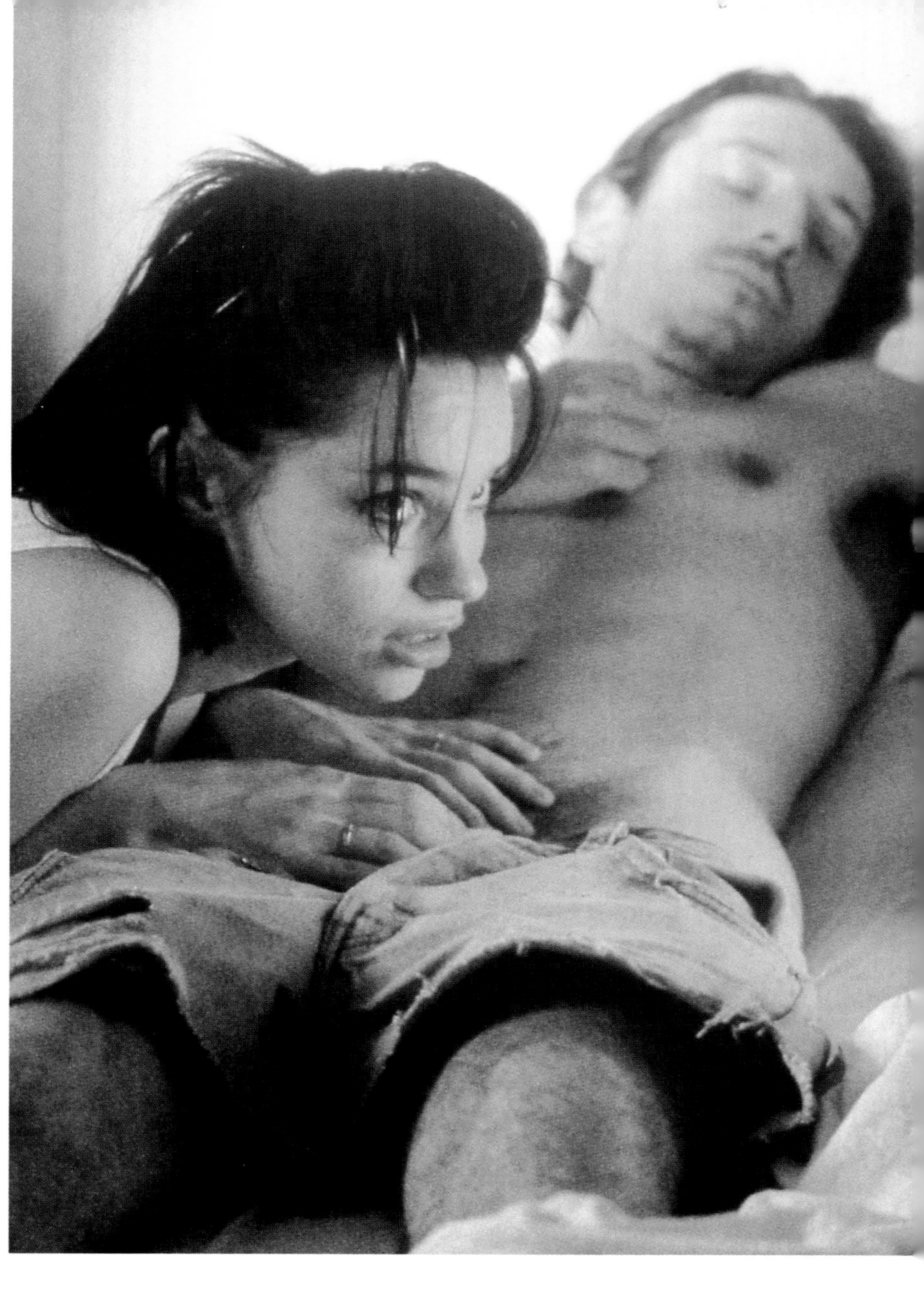

fulfilment. Betty's uninhibited lust does not drain Zorg; it inspires his passion and creativity, as in the scene where he kisses up the full length of her nude body while she tells him about her dream that his novel will get published. But when Zorg's work keeps being rejected and she is unable to get pregnant, Betty goes insane, and in her madness she threatens, like a femme fatale, to take him down with her. She knocks him into a bathtub and throws herself into a river. When Zorg finally receives word that his book will be published, Betty is in an insane asylum, unable to appreciate that her dream for him has come true.

Still from 'Betty Blue' (1986)
Betty has an almost carnivorous connection to Zorg (Jean-Hugues Anglade), with whom she is madly in love.

Homosexuality / Lesbianism / Transvestism / Transsexuality

In the 1934 Hollywood film *Wonder Bar*, a man and a woman are dancing. Another fellow approaches, tapping the man on the shoulder to ask, "May I cut in?" It is the classic dance-floor scene, only this time movie audiences were taken by surprise when the two men dance off together. As screenwriter Anita Loos once commented, "Men no longer prefer blondes. Today gentlemen seem to prefer gentlemen." The first film to deal directly with homosexuality was *Anders als die Andern* (1919), where Conrad Veidt meets Reinhold Schünzel at a gay dance, takes him home and (briefly) caresses his (fully clothed) chest. That was all, but it was enough: the taboo against showing male-on-male sexual contact had been broken, at least by implication.

Certain gay films that came later continued to develop the possibilities of Eros by suggestion, even when censorship did not demand such indirection. In *Pink Narcissus* (1971), a butterfly emerging from its cocoon and held near a man's bulging crotch serves as a metaphor for his coming out, and the ecstasy of orgasm is implied in the image of a Roman candle protruding from a man's trouser fly and sending out sparks in *Fireworks* (1947). In *Caravaggio* (1986), it is clear that painter Nigel Terry's interest is more than professional when he places a coin between his lips and makes male model Sean Bean "kiss" him to claim payment. And two prisoners in separate cells share more than a cigarette in *Un Chant d'Amour* (1950) when one man blows smoke through a straw in the wall into the other's mouth.

The mere suggestion of a kiss can bring about an erotic frisson beyond that of actual snogging. There is a pervasive homoeroticism in *Interview with the Vampire* (1994), as in the moment when Latin lover/vampire Antonio Banderas comes close to pressing his mouth to Brad Pitt, or in the scene where Pitt swoons under the hungry lips of heartthrob Tom Cruise at his throat. In *My Own Private Idaho* (1993), mere proximity carries an extra charge in the scenes where River Phoenix straddles Keanu Reeves on the back of a motorcycle. Sexily narcoleptic Phoenix longs to wake up in the arms of his closest friend. It is interesting to note that actor Reeves has said, "I'm not heterosexual and I'm not homosexual. I'm just sexual." In *Dude, Where's My Car?* (2000), hunky stoners Ashton Kutcher and Seann William Scott are ostensibly straight, but they keep passing out and waking up next to each other in various states of undress. Commenting on these scantily clad scenes, actor Kutcher has said that "I wanted to wear the tighty whities because it's funnier. Well, my hog

Still from 'Jamón, jamón' (1992)
Javier Bardem gives a hammy performance as a sexy meat delivery man.

Repressed Desire

Page 60 Top Left: 'Merry Christmas, Mr Lawrence' (1983) The intimate connection between prisoner of war David Bowie and camp commander Ryuichi Sakamoto runs counter to the warlike relations they are expected to have.

Page 60 Centre Left: 'The Sergeant' (1968) John Phillip Law gets a furious kiss from self-hating homosexual Rod Steiger.

Page 60 Bottom Left: 'Interview with the Vampire' (1994) Enemy vampires Brad Pitt and Antonio Banderas come close to giving in to their bloodlust for one another.

Page 60 Top Centre: 'Women in Love' (1969) The nude wrestling match between Oliver Reed and Alan Bates. Male genitals were bared for the first time in a mainstream film – and in a homoerotic context.

Page 60 Bottom Centre: 'Point Break' (1991) Homoerotic overtones add to the excitement for skydivers Keanu Reeves and Patrick Swayze. "All great American films are love stories between two men," says Brad Lucas.

"They can't censor the gleam in my eye."

Actor Charles Laughton

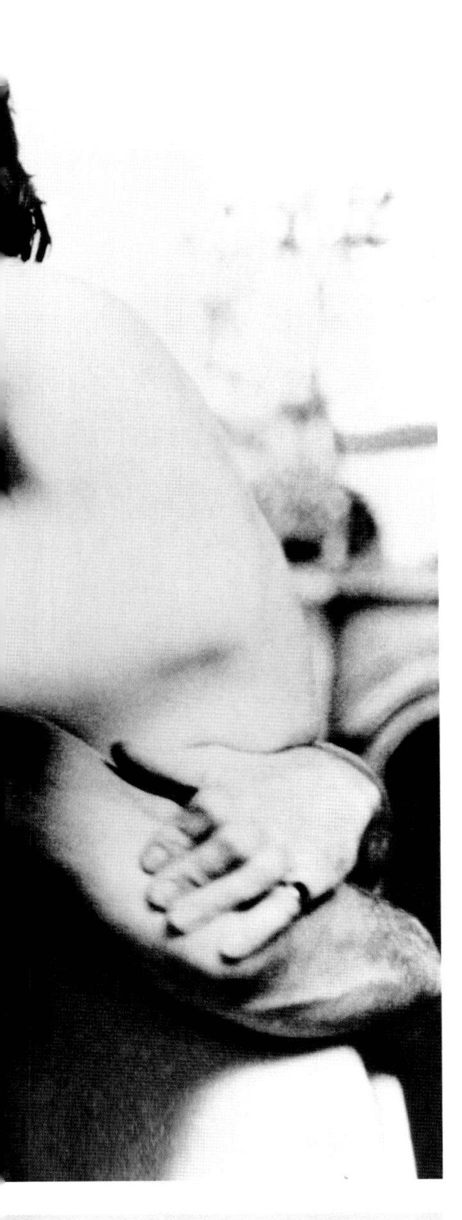

Explicit Desire

Top Right: 'Fox and His Friends' (1975) Upper-class snob Karlheinz Böhm exploits the bodies of working-class men.

Center Right: 'Hustler White' (1996) A blond gay hustler has a taste for black men in this film from director Bruce LaBruce that plays with racial stereotypes.

Page 62 Top: 'L'Homme blessé' (1983) Jean-Hugues Anglade will have Vittorio Mezzogiorno one way or the other.

Page 62 Bottom: 'Querelle' (1982) Roger Bataille gives Brad Davis a reach-around in a world of pulsing colours and desires.

Page 63 Top: 'Saudade' (2003) Hendrick Scheider is embraced by Aldri Anunciação. The two finance their vacation by webcasting scenes of their lovemaking on the beaches of Brazil.

Page 63 Bottom: On the set of 'Querelle' (1982) Brad Davis looks on while director Rainer Werner Fassbinder (in glasses) demonstrates how to give a gay embrace to Hanno Pöschl. (And note the placement of the cigarette.)

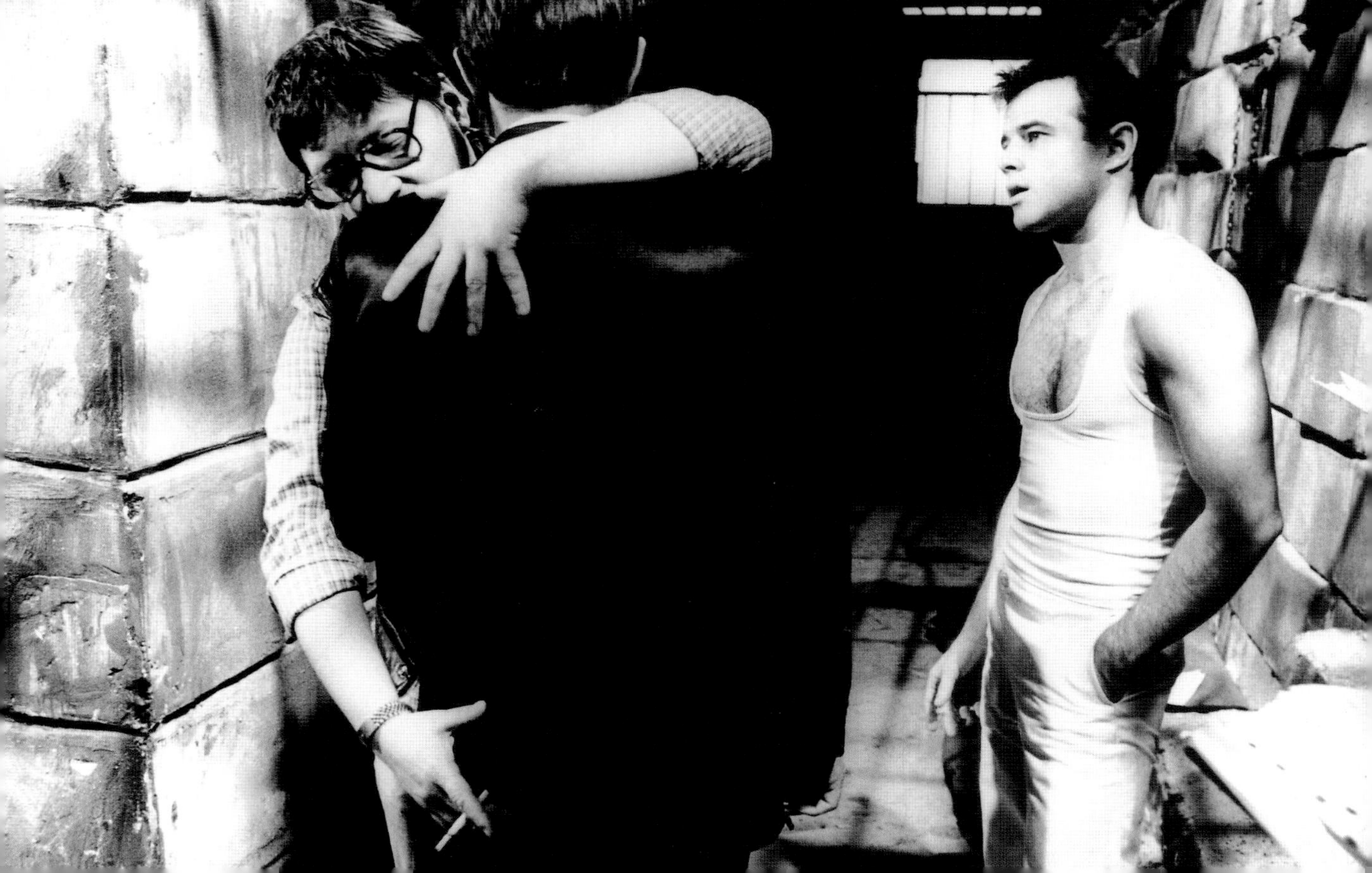

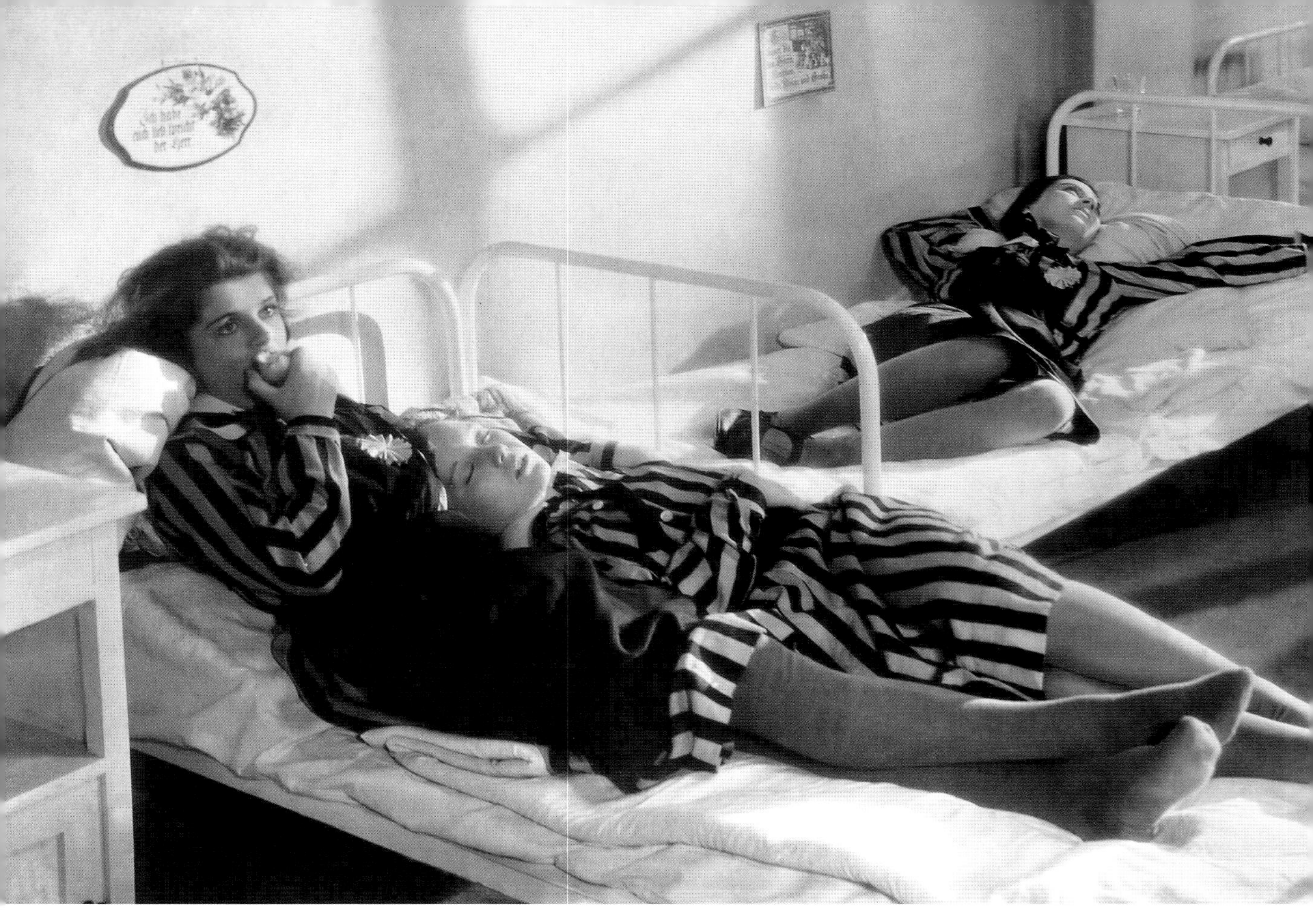

ABOVE
Still from 'Mädchen in Uniform' (1931)
Budding eroticism among Hertha Thiele (eating the fruit) and other students at a girls' boarding school.

RIGHT
Still from 'The Rainbow' (1989)
Swim coach Amanda Donohoe gives Sammi Davis a sensual massage.

"I can't think of a single movie that can't be improved with a lesbian sex scene."

Steve Zahn, ***Freak Talks About Sex*** **(1999)**

ABOVE
Still from 'Emmanuelle' (1974)
The tennis match may have ended, but the game continues between Jeanne Colletin and Sylvia Kristel at a country club.

LEFT
Still from 'Lust for a Vampire' (1971)
Sapphic bloodsucker Yutte Stensgaard gives a toothsome kiss to Judy Matheson. "Every vampire movie needs to have some girl-on-girl action," as producer Keith Border has said.

was hanging out, and it was, like, showing through my underwear. So they made me put on these brown shorts." "This movie is homoerotic enough as it is," said director Danny Leiner. "We don't need you in your tighty whities." In *American Pie 2* (2001), two women promise that horny hetero buddies Seann William Scott and Jason Biggs will get to see some hot lesbian action if the two guys are willing to kiss each other first – and they do. The buddies' lip-lock has a powerful homophobic/homoerotic charge.

Still from 'M. Butterfly' (1993)
French diplomat Jeremy Irons pretends not to realize that his lover, a Chinese opera singer, is a man in drag (John Lone).

The first romantic kiss between men in a mainstream film had occurred in *Sunday, Bloody Sunday* (1971) when Murray Head comes home to Peter Finch, who takes him into his arms. As director John Schlesinger has said, "I wanted them to embrace and kiss quite passionately as lovers but not to make a big deal of it. It should happen as though it happened every time they met. It was not, 'here are these twilight people driven to each other with these terrible appetites which somehow they slake with their impure lips.' It was, 'Hi honey, what's for lunch?' or 'what's for dinner?'" But in other films, homoerotic desire is felt as too great a threat to sexual identity and the established social order for a gay kiss not to be explosive. When Rod Steiger as *The Sergeant* (1968) on a military base struggles to overcome years of repression by planting a violent kiss on the mouth of a young recruit (John Phillip Law), his rejection by the other man leads him to put a gun to his own head. And in *Merry Christmas, Mr. Lawrence* (1983), when prisoner of war David Bowie kisses camp commander Ryuichi Sakamoto in front of all the guards and prisoners, the public revelation of Sakamoto's hidden homoerotic desire does not bring love instead of war, but is viewed as a sign of weakness and a stain on his honour as a warrior. Some theatre audiences booed the kiss between Michael Caine and Christopher Reeve in *Deathtrap* (1982), which became known as "the ten-million-dollar kiss" because this was the amount of money that the film was said to have lost due to its gay kissing scene, but by the time of *In & Out* (1997) audiences were cheering the scene where Tom Selleck gives Kevin Kline an extended and enthusiastic kiss in an effort to get him to come out as gay. Among the most passionate gay kisses is the one in *My Beautiful Laundrette* (1985) where blond punker Daniel Day-Lewis celebrates the laundry he has opened with Pakistani Gordon Warnecke by dribbling champagne from his mouth into his lover's.

Lesbian kisses also have a long and varied history on film. In *Mädchen in Uniform* (1931), all the girls in a boarding school await the moment each night when beloved teacher Dorothea Wieck comes to their bed to give them a goodnight kiss on their foreheads, but one girl throws her arms around the teacher's neck and Wieck kisses her on the lips. In *Morocco* (1930), cabaret singer Marlene Dietrich, dressed in a man's tuxedo and top hat, suddenly turns to a woman in the audience, looks her over, and gives her a kiss on the mouth, while Greta Garbo as *Queen Christina* (1933) dresses in velvet trousers and kisses her lady-in-waiting. When warned that she will die an old maid, Garbo replies, "I have no intention to. I shall die a bachelor." Joan Crawford once said about acting in a film with Garbo, "If there was ever a time in my life when I might have become a lesbian, that was it."

Wesley Snipes: "You most certainly won't be going out with Mr. Bobby Ray."
John Leguizamo: "Why not? We have a lot in common."
Wesley Snipes: "Oh yes, for starters, the same business in between your legs."

***To Wong Foo, Thanks for Everything! Julie Newmar* (1995)**

Audience ambivalence about the thrill and the threat of Sapphic love and active female desire is made manifest in the figure of the lesbian vampire whose kisses can kill. In *Twins of Evil* (1971), lusty and busty Madeleine Collinson has writhing peasant girl Luan Peters chained to a wall, but then the victim seems to respond to the vampire's advances and the two almost kiss – before the red-lipped Collinson starts sucking on Peters' breasts. In *The Vampire Lovers* (1970), feral Ingrid Pitt

ABOVE

Still from 'Boys Don't Cry' (1999)

Chloë Sevigny finds that sensitive cowboy transvestite Hilary Swank pleases her more than macho men ever have.

LEFT

Still from 'The Crying Game' (1992)

Stephen Rea falls in love with Jaye Davidson and then is shocked to discover that "she" has male genitals.

ABOVE
Still from 'The Damned' (1969)
Helmut Berger gives a decadent performance in drag inspired by Marlene Dietrich's nightclub act in 'The Blue Angel' (1930).

ABOVE RIGHT
Still from 'The Key' (1983)
Wife Stefania Sandrelli is helped to overcome her repression by kinky cross-dresser husband Frank Finlay.

OPPOSITE
Publicity still for 'The Rocky Horror Picture Show' (1975)
As the "sweet transvestite from Transsexual, Transylvania", Tim Curry worships at the altar of the muscular male physique.

comes to Madeline Smith's bed each night, opening the woman's nightgown to nuzzle and nibble at her bare breasts. Smith remembers these nocturnal visits only as a sensual nightmare, which she later recounts to Pitt: "A cat comes, sits at the foot of my bed, and it reaches toward me, and I try to scream but my throat is strangled. And it lies across me, warm and heavy, and I feel its fur in my mouth, and I retch with fear, and then – it turns into you!" *Vampyros Lesbos* (*Las Vampiras*, 1971) has fatal beauty Soledad Miranda, clad in black and wearing a red scarf, strip the white gown off blonde Ewa Strömberg and fall to feeding on her neck, whereas it is blonde femme Catherine Deneuve who exhibits *The Hunger* (1983) for butch Susan Sarandon when the latter spills red sherry on her white T-shirt. Deneuve initiates contact by touching Sarandon's shoulder and neck, prompting her to take off her shirt so that Deneuve can touch her breasts. Later, in bed, Deneuve leads in giving a love-bite to Sarandon's arm, which the latter then reciprocates by sucking on Deneuve's arm in a kind of vampire-lesbian 69.

If *The Hunger* shows Sapphic desire beginning to come out from the fear and sadomasochism with which it was often associated in the lesbian vampire film, other movies went even further in showing that lesbian lust could also be mutual love. In *Lianna* (1982), two women sit on a sofa and engage their lips in verbal foreplay, sharing sexual fantasies then living one out in bed, as breathless whispers are heard on the soundtrack during their lovemaking. Joan Chen puts her mouth to Anne Heche's breasts in *Wild Side* (1995), and Heche's passionate response is symbolized by the bright red walls of the executive washroom in which they are having sex, while the mutual love between two women in *Desert Hearts* (1985) is figured in the mirror image of their breasts touching as they make out in bed. The lower body is the focus in *French Twist* (*Gazon Maudit*, 1995), where Josiane Balasko fondles Victoria Abril's leg under a table in one scene, and in another Abril reclines on a sofa, showing off her legs under a short skirt to Balasko. Finally, *Bound* (1996) explores several erogenous zones in a sofa scene where Jennifer Tilly touches Gina

ABOVE

Still from 'Myra Breckinridge' (1970)
Transsexual Raquel Welch prepares to rape macho stud Roger Herren with a dildo in order to further her goal: "the destruction of the American male in all its particulars".

RIGHT

Still from 'Myra Breckinridge' (1970)
Uncle Buck (John Huston) gasps as Myra (Raquel Welch) finds a dramatic way to reveal that she was once Myron. She says, "your fag nephew became your niece two years ago in Copenhagen and is now free as a bird and happy in being the most extraordinary woman in the world!"

Gershon's hand to her breast, then moistens Gershon's finger with her mouth and places it between her thighs. Later, it is Gershon who receives Tilly's finger inserted between the lips of her mouth.

As we saw with Dietrich in *Morocco* and Garbo in *Queen Christina*, a lesbian identification sometimes involves cross-dressing as a man. In *Boys Don't Cry* (1999), Hilary Swank stuffs her crotch, tapes down her breasts, and dons a cowboy hat to pass as male. But despite the macho look, she retains a feminine capacity for empathy which leads Chloë Sevigny to fall for her. Trans-gendered Swank refuses to limit herself to one sex role and re-creates herself as an ideal combination of vigour and compassion. In their outdoor lovemaking scene, Swank's androgynous appeal brings Sevigny to orgasm, enabling the other woman as well to find her own sexuality in defiance of social convention. Director Kimberly Peirce explains why she holds Sevigny's ecstatic face in close-up during that climactic moment: "If I could've gotten the camera down [her] throat past her tonsils and then pulled out, I would have, because it would've been hopefully what it's like to have that biggest orgasm, that orgasm that creates oneself. So it's echoing…throughout that scene, throughout that town, throughout the country. It's a rebel yell."

Not everyone is as open to the experience of being freed from gender roles and sexual conventions. When female-to-male transvestite John Lazar tries to entice Michael Blodgett by showing him his womanly breasts in *Beyond the Valley of the Dolls* (1970), Blodgett is thoroughly repelled, and Stephen Rea is sickened enough to vomit at the discovery of male genitals on the body of the gorgeously feminine Jaye Davidson with whom he was about to make love in *The Crying Game* (1992). Nevertheless, some trans-gendered characters are able to take pride in the thought that they embody the best of both sexes. In *Stonewall* (1995), transvestite Guillermo Diaz refuses to be "cured" of his condition, boasting to his psychiatrist that he lives in a "state between maleness and femaleness" called "fabulousness", while in *Car Wash* (1976) snap queen Antonio Fargas tells off one of his macho tormentors with the devastating line, "Honey, I'm more man than you'll ever be and more woman than you'll ever get."

For some male characters, transvestism can help them discover a feminine side to themselves. In *Some Like It Hot* (1959), while dressed in drag, Tony Curtis is able to identify with Marilyn Monroe's pain when another man leaves her. By helping her realize that no man is worth crying over, Curtis proves that he himself is worthy of her love. In *Thunderbolt and Lightfoot* (1974), Jeff Bridges puts on women's clothes as a disguise, but before robbing the bank, he looks at himself in the mirror and thinks, "Oh, you sexy bitch, I'd even go with you myself." Actor John Lithgow put it more seriously and eloquently when speaking of the pleasure he found in playing a transsexual in *The World According to Garp* (1982): "Sitting alone in my trailer, all dressed up in drag, I would run my hands over the strange, artificial curves of my body, look at myself in the mirror, smile and wink. Boy-John and girl-John were sharing a secret, a sexy joke that no one else was in on."

Among the profoundest explorations of gender-bending and sexual disorientation are the scenes in *Performance* (1970) where Mick Jagger dresses macho James Fox in women's clothes and a blonde wig, and where Anita Pallenberg uses a mirror to reflect one of her breasts onto Fox's chest so that he appears as half-man and half-woman. As a result, Fox overcomes some of his homophobia, finding that his feminine side is attracted to the boyish body of Michèle Breton and that he is even willing to share a bed with effeminate Jagger. And in *The Rocky Horror*

"My taste includes both snails and oysters."

Laurence Olivier to Tony Curtis in *Spartacus* (1960)

Still from 'Private School' (1983)
Betsy Russell pretends that she is fooled by Matthew Modine's drag disguise and deliberately drives him crazy by taking her clothes off in front of this other "girl".

Still from 'Law of Desire' (1987)
Juan (Miguel Molina, top) is entwined with Pablo (Eusebio Poncela) in an iconic image of same-sex intimacy.

Picture Show (1975), sweet transvestite Tim Curry seduces both female and male members of a straight newlywed couple by sneaking into their separate bedrooms at night, going down on them in the dark, and bringing them so much pleasure that they don't want him to stop – even after they discover he is not their mate. Curry's sexual and sartorial daring proves infectious: by the end of the film, both the bride and the groom are dressed like Curry in black corsets, fishnet stockings and stiletto heels for a wildly uninhibited dance number whose orgiastic climax has all the characters making love to each other in a swimming pool.

Director Pedro Almodóvar's *Law of Desire* (*La Ley del deseo*, 1987) challenged audiences with the complexity of its gay and trans-gendered characters. Carmen Maura plays Tina, a male-to-female transsexual who had a sex change to please her father, with whom she was incestuously involved. However, since he abandoned her, she has grown increasingly dissatisfied with her female form. The film does allow her one moment of ecstasy in a scene where, walking down a Madrid street on a hot night, she asks a cleaning man to turn his hose on her. As the jet of water arches across the street to drench her clinging orange-knit dress, she runs her hands over her curves and writhes in pure enjoyment.

Tina's brother, Pablo (Eusebio Poncela), is a gay film-maker, and we hear him give directions to a young male actor during the shooting of a bedroom masturbation scene. First Pablo has the actor strip down to his white underwear, rub his crotch against the glass of a full-body mirror, and kiss his own image before the young man is instructed to remove his briefs, kneel on a bed and masturbate while

Kevin Munday: "Are you sure you like boys?"
Marya Delver: "Soft centres, hard centres – I like all the chocolates in the box."

Better Than Chocolate **(1998)**

saying, "Fuck me." The scene reflects director Pablo's own narcissistic sexuality and his desire to bend others to his will, and the actor in the scene balks at taking up a purely passive position before the domineering director. However, another man named Antonio (Antonio Banderas) is so excited by the scene that, after seeing it in the finished film, he rushes to the theatre lavatory to masturbate while repeating the actor's words. Antonio then begins a sexual relationship with Pablo, inviting the director to penetrate him but also taking an active role in insisting that Pablo love and be faithful to him. In this way, Antonio both fulfils Pablo's fantasies and challenges his narcissism.

Still from 'Law of Desire' (1987)
The more experienced Pablo introduces Antonio (Antonio Banderas) to gay love.

Richard Ruccolo: "I always thought Ken was gay."
Dan Bucatinsky: "He was when I got through with him."

All Over the Guy **(2001)**

Virginity / Incestuous Desire

In the late 1930s, Graham Greene was sued for libel for suggesting that a certain female child star excited prurient interest in male viewers: 'Infancy with Shirley Temple is a disguise. Her appeal is more secret and more adult. She is a complete totsy. Watch the way she measures a man with agile studio eyes, with dimpled depravity…Some of her popularity seems to rest on a coquetry quite as mature as [Claudette] Colbert's and an oddly precocious body as voluptuous in gray flannel trousers as [Marlene] Dietrich's.' Greene's claim does not seem so outrageous when you consider that in *Kiddin' Hollywood* (1932), which is part of the *Baby Burlesk* series of one-reelers, four-year-old Shirley Temple is provocatively dressed and posed as Morelegs Sweet Trick in a parody of Marlene Dietrich from *The Blue Angel* (1930). In *War Babies* (1932), Temple plays a French nightclub performer being plied with lollipops from little boys dressed as soldiers, one of whom undoes her diaper pin and licks it.

Child-women who blur the line between virgin and vamp have a double appeal, the freshness of innocence combined with a willingness to be naughty. From one perspective, they allow adults to relive the first, fresh stirrings of desire. From another angle, child-women offer the thrill of corrupting an innocent. In *Baby Doll* (1956), Karl Malden leers through a peephole bored in the wall at his 19-year-old 'child-bride' curled up in a crib, desiring her but having agreed not to possess her until she turns 20. While this scene seems driven by the husband's lechery, another is focused on budding female desire. As a male seducer rocks Baby Doll higher and higher in a swing, her face conveys the sense that she is reaching orgasm. According to Carroll Baker, who played Baby Doll, "In my efforts to be real in the sexually evocative scenes of the film, I worked myself into a combustible, near-volcanic state of desire... I was still smouldering after the 'takes', so that if anyone inadvertently touched me it was difficult to suppress a moan. I got really worried when I couldn't sit in the make-up chair without fear of climaxing."

The world's best-known child-woman is Lolita, heroine of Vladimir Nabokov's 1955 novel. There is an interesting connection with film history in the fact that the real-life model for Nabokov's Lolita may have been Lilita McMurray, the 15-year-old child-bride of Charlie Chaplin. Chaplin was forced to marry the girl to avoid being jailed for having had sex with a minor, and he was later sued for divorce on the grounds that his request for oral sex constituted mental cruelty. Another source for

Publicity still for 'Lolita' (1962)
The power relationship between Humbert Humbert (James Mason) and under-age Lolita (Sue Lyon) is made clear in this still. According to author Vladimir Nabokov, Lolita has 'a tender dreamy childishness and a kind of eerie vulgarity'.

"She's half child."
"Not the half that shows."

Talking about Marilyn Monroe in *Monkey Business* (1952)

ABOVE
Still from 'Baby Doll' (1956)
Child-woman Carroll Baker sucking her "thumb".

LEFT
Still from 'Pretty Baby' (1978)
Young Brooke Shields (in foreground) watches while Keith Carradine talks with her prostitute-mother Susan Sarandon. Shields later said, "Sure I knew what was going on with the sex scenes... I just didn't say so."

OPPOSITE TOP
Still from 'Lolita' (1962)
Lolita seduces a nervous Humbert with lessons she learned at Camp Climax.

OPPOSITE BOTTOM
Still from 'Lolita' (1997)
Dominique Swain in the remake of 'Lolita'. 'In a sense, Lolita is always something of a devil's child, even against her will. She lures, however innocently, grown men into forbidden paths.' (Marianne Sinclair, 'Hollywood Lolitas')

ABOVE
Still from 'American Beauty' (1999)
A father has a fantasy of his daughter's friend (Mina Suvari) lying in a bed of rose petals, ready for deflowering.

RIGHT
Still from 'Exotica' (1994)
Mia Kirshner performs her schoolgirl striptease for a customer. "What is it that gives a schoolgirl her special innocence?" asks the emcee.

OPPOSITE
Stills from 'The Blue Lagoon' (1980)
Christopher Atkins and Brooke Shields discover their sexuality while marooned on an island paradise far removed from the guilt of adult society. For critic Pauline Kael, having the couple be so 'clean and innocent' ended up 'emptying them of any dramatic interest. Watching them is about as exciting as looking into a fishbowl waiting for guppies to mate.'

"I'm a young virgin in Italy and I want my sexual awakening – and I want it now!"

Georgina Cates, ***Stiff Upper Lips*** (2000)

Still from 'Tea and Sympathy' (1956)
Housemaster's wife Deborah Kerr helps to 'mother' boarding-school boy John Kerr into manhood.

Still from 'The Graduate' (1967)
College boy Benjamin (Dustin Hoffman) is seduced by the stockinged leg of older woman Mrs. Robinson (Anne Bancroft). Bancroft was actually only six years older than Hoffman.

"When a man of forty falls in love with a girl of twenty, it isn't her youth he is seeking but his own."

Screenwriter Lenore Coffee

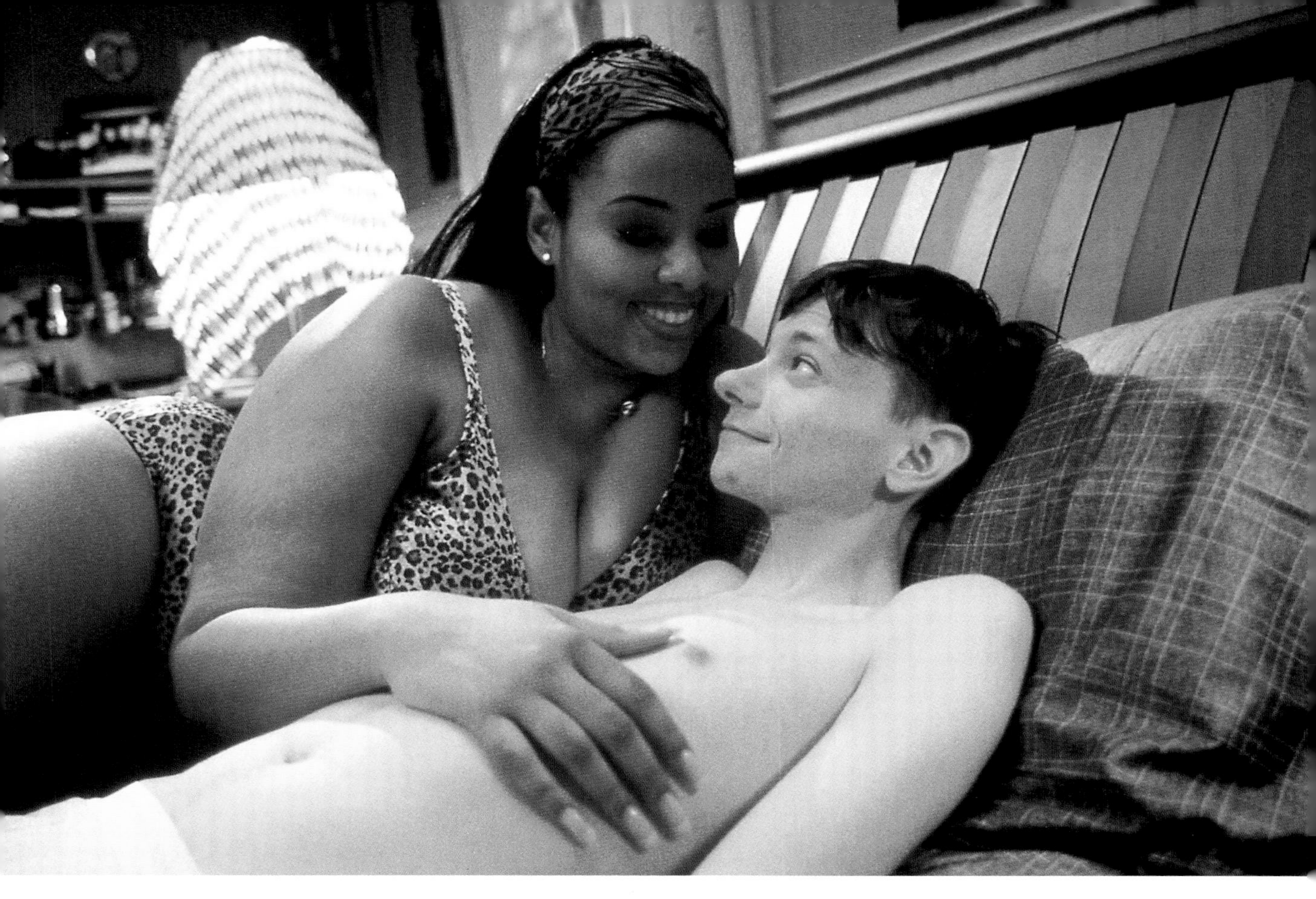

ABOVE

Still from 'Road Trip' (2000)

Black sorority sister Mia Amber Davis is charmed by nerdy D.J. Qualls into helping him lose his virginity.

LEFT

Still from 'Pretty Maids All in a Row' (1971)

Teenager John David Carlson is happy to have Angie Dickinson help him find the bar of soap that has fallen between his legs.

ABOVE
Still from 'Harold and Maude' (1971)
Death-obsessed teenager Bud Cort finds a reason to live in his romance with fearless 79-year-old Ruth Gordon.

RIGHT
Still from 'Sitcom' (1998)
Évelyne Dandry attempts her own 'cure' for her son Adrien de Van's homosexuality.

the name "Lolita" is the word "lollipop", like the red one that Sue Lyon sucks while wearing her heart-shaped sunglasses in the poster for Stanley Kubrick's 1962 film of *Lolita*. To avoid a Condemned rating from the Catholic Legion of Decency, which would have spelled box-office disaster, Kubrick raised the age of Lolita from 12 to 14 in his film and toned down the novel's sensuality. For his 1997 remake of *Lolita*, Adrian Lyne also faced strong resistance from conservative groups, particularly in America where the murder of six-year-old beauty-pageant queen JonBenet Ramsey and the passage of the Child Pornography Prevention Act created a climate in which Lyne could not find a US distributor for the film. (It eventually aired on cable television.) Lyne's film features a scene in which Dominique Swain (Lolita) sits on Jeremy Irons' lap in a rocking chair. At first she is, like a child, engrossed in the comics she is reading, but as he rocks her to and fro, an adult expression crosses her face and she moans in the throes of orgasm.

In *Pretty Baby* (1978), Brooke Shields plays a 12-year-old girl whose mother is a prostitute in a New Orleans brothel. The film was denounced by some as child pornography for such scenes as the one where Shields is exhibited to the johns on a silver platter and has her virginity auctioned off to the highest bidder. David Carradine, as a man who photographs the 'working girls', would seem to be as lecherous as the other men, but then he offers Shields his own home as a safe haven

Gene Kelly: "You're 40, he's 22. Do you have to marry him?"
Liv Ullmann: "As opposed to what?"
Gene Kelly: "Couldn't you just adopt him?"

40 Carats (1973)

from the brothel and he treats her with fatherly tenderness and respect. However, when Carradine goes on to propose marriage to the girl, we are left to wonder whether his special interest in her is paternal or prurient. Did he save her from the brothel only so that he could possess her himself? In *Exotica* (1994), Bruce Greenwood is obsessively drawn to a nightclub where he watches 'schoolgirl' stripper Mia Kirshner remove her white shirt, plaid skirt and knee socks. Greenwood's daughter was murdered, and by visiting Kirshner, who is his niece, he gets to bring his daughter alive again and imagine himself as her protector. However, in watching her schoolgirl striptease, Greenwood also puts himself in the killer's place and violates a child. The line between fatherly devotion and incestuous desire is similarly blurred in *American Beauty* (1999), where midlife-crisis-ridden Kevin Spacey has a fantasy of his daughter's best friend, Mina Suvari, lying naked in a bed of rose petals. However, in a moment of moral triumph, Spacey later resists the temptation to deflower her.

Interestingly, films dealing with quasi-incestuous relations between older women and younger men tend to be less emotionally fraught than their father-daughter equivalents. In *Love Strange Love* (*Amor Estranho Amor*, 1982), Marcelo Ribeiro plays a pubescent boy who is wide-eyed witness to a variety of sexual encounters in a brothel and whose growing desires are finally satisfied in a tender sexual initiation

ABOVE
Still from 'Murmur of the Heart' (1971)
After being left by her lover, Lea Massari turns to her son Benoît Ferreux for sexual comfort.

LEFT
Still from 'Luna' (1979)
Troubled son Matthew Barry seeks solace by drawing close to his opera diva mother Jill Clayburgh.

Penelope Wilton: "A girl that age, still a virgin – it's absurd!"
Jonathan Pryce: "I was still a virgin at her age."
Penelope Wilton: "But that's my whole point, don't you see? So was I. Is there to be no progress?"

Carrington **(1995)**

Still from 'Summer with Monika' (1953)
Harriet Andersson spends summer nights under the stars with her lover on one of Sweden's archipelagos. For 1953, this truly was 'a picture for wide screens and broad minds', as its ad said.

Paul Sonkkila: "Is that pornography or art?"
Linda Hunt: "If it's in focus, it's pornography. If it's out of focus, it's art."

The Year of Living Dangerously **(1982)**

ABOVE

Still from 'Tendres cousines' (1980)

Young Thierry Tevini enjoys a roll in the hay with servant girl Anne Fontaine during a luminous summer of sexual awakening.

LEFT

Still from 'A Night in the Life of Jimmy Reardon' (1988)

River Phoenix puts the moves on Kristin Weithas in this film about coming of age in the 1960s, when having sex in the car was often the only way to go.

ABOVE
Still from 'Kids' (1995)
Girl #1 (Sarah Henderson) loses her virginity to smooth-talker Telly (Leo Fitzpatrick): "I like you. I think you're beautiful. I want to make you happy."

RIGHT
Still from 'Kids' (1995)
Horny teenage skateboarders loose on the streets of New York City.

by his own prostitute-mother. (An actress who has a seductive scene with the boy, Xuxa Meneghel, later became a children's television star and attempted to take all prints and videos of the film out of circulation.) Headmaster's wife Deborah Kerr provides kissing lessons and more to a grateful John Kerr after other boys torment him for being unmanly in *Tea and Sympathy* (1956), while in *Get Out Your Handkerchiefs* (*Préparez vos mouchoirs*, 1978) Carole Laure gives sexual encouragement to ostracized youth Riton by singling him out for kisses in front of the other boys in the dorm and by taking him into her bed. The loving 'mothers' in these films are not presented as entirely selfless: Deborah Kerr seems more attracted to the sensitive boy than to her macho husband, and Carole Laure is able to fulfil her desire to be a mother. In *Murmur of the Heart* (*Le Souffle au coeur*, 1971), the satisfaction is mutual: son Benoît Ferreux becomes his mother's comforter in bed after her lover leaves her, while she (Lea Massari) ensures that his first time will be with a devoted and uninhibited woman.

Incest is presented as more problematic in *The Graduate* (1967), where the relationship between college boy Dustin Hoffman and his mother's friend Anne Bancroft starts out as endearingly comic ("Mrs. Robinson, you're trying to seduce me. Aren't you?"), but then becomes tragic as she battens onto him like a vampire and threatens to ruin his romance with her daughter. Another case where adult desire becomes an imposition on the young can be found in *Sweet Sweetback's Baadasssss Song* (1971). Director Melvin Van Peebles cast his own 13-year-old son Mario in the role of young Sweetback, who proves himself to be a stud in the scene where he loses his virginity to an older female prostitute at the beginning of the film. Years later, grown-up son Mario himself became a director and made an autobiographical film, *Baadasssss!* (2003), which reveals something of the psychic cost inflicted on the young Mario when his father put him together with an older woman in that disturbingly explicit scene.

"It's bad protocol to reject tongue, unless it's a scene in which you're kissing your dad. If the other person clenches their teeth, you just say, 'Okay, they don't want that much cinema vérité.'"

Actress Jennifer Tilly

Still from 'Kids' (1995)
Darcy (Yakira Peguero) responds to the advances of Telly as they sit at the edge of a swimming pool. She will be his next sexual conquest.

The director who has been most heavily criticized for his 'exploitative' depictions of teenage sexuality is Larry Clark. Clark's film *Kids* (1995) was shot in cinéma-vérité style, but some have charged that his claims of documentary realism are really an excuse for prurience and paedophilia. One way to defend *Kids* would be to see it as a cautionary tale similar to the old 'vice' and 'sex hygiene' films that warned about the dangers of venereal disease. The film follows Jennie (Chloë Sevigny), who contracted the HIV virus when she lost her virginity to Telly (Leo Fitzpatrick), in her quest to find him before he infects another girl. However, when she does finally locate him, he is already having sex with Darcy (Yakira Peguero). Jennie gives up, passing out due to drugs and despair, and then to top it all off, she is raped when Telly's friend Casper (Justin Pierce) takes advantage of her helplessness, possibly infecting himself in the process.

If *Kids* warns that sex can be a fall into death, it also romanticizes the time before that fall when teens are first discovering the world of sensuality. The film opens on an idyllic scene in which Telly is kissing a girl (Sarah Henderson) on a flowered bedspread in her room. Telly may be a nefarious seducer, but the film draws us into the girl's dreamy perspective with intimate close-ups and sensual sounds of their French kissing. After sex, Telly has his friend Casper sniff his finger, and Casper exclaims in wonder, "Smells like butterscotch." Later, girls at a pyjama party believe enough in the possibility of sexual fulfilment that they thrill to a story about a boy with "magic fingers". Thus, *Kids* is as much about teenagers' innocent faith in sensual pleasure as it about their fall from innocence into disease and death.

Jeremy Northam: "Do you believe in love at first sight?"
Parker Posey: "I just lost my virginity, not my mind!"

The Misadventures of Margaret **(2000)**

Voyeurism / Exhibitionism / Masturbation

"What did voyeurs do before there was film?" asks director John Waters. Movie lovers have long recognized the voyeuristic potential of film, with stars undressing in intimate close-up before audiences who sit in a darkened theatre and who watch without being seen, engrossed in fantasies which feed their imagination. When the film censors who wrote the 1930 Production Code stipulated that scenes of 'undressing' and 'passion' should be avoided, particularly ones that involve 'lustful embraces' and 'handling of the body', it was because they knew that such scenes tend to 'arouse or excite the passions of the ordinary spectator'. (These passions were thought to be 'subversive to the interest of society, and a peril to the human race' – despite the fact that there would be no human race without them.)

That the 'handling of the body' on-screen can lead to self-fondling off-screen is something that the movies themselves show us. In *Amarcord* (1972), a group of boys screams out the name of screen goddess Jean Harlow as they masturbate in a car, which is bouncing up and down and has its headlights flickering on and off. In *The Dreamers* (2003), it is Marlene Dietrich that Louis Garrel is dreaming of as he brings himself to climax on her wall photo. And, from the female perspective, Kim Basinger finds that watching slides in a screening room moves her to self-stimulation in *9 1/2 Weeks* (1986).

Many of the earliest films were essentially peepshows where voyeurs could see flashes of temptingly exposed flesh. *La Puce* (1897) is a filmed version of a music-hall striptease act in which a woman removes her garments one by one while supposedly searching for a flea. In *The Hypocrites* (1915), the alibi for nudity is allegory as a woman proudly represents 'The Naked Truth'. This was a little bit too much truth for the mayor of Boston, who demanded that clothes be painted onto the lady, frame by frame. In period films set during prudish times, the showing of just a little skin can be immensely arousing, as when Harvey Keitel pokes his finger through a hole in Holly Hunter's stocking in *The Piano* (1993), or when the four buttons of Michelle Pfeiffer's glove are slowly undone and her wrist is laid bare by Daniel Day-Lewis in *The Age of Innocence* (1993). Rita Hayworth's slow removal of a long black glove in *Gilda* (1946) is enough to suggest a whole-body striptease, and Claudette Colbert proves that "the limb is mightier than the thumb" when she gets a car to stop just by showing a little leg while hitchhiking with Clark Gable in *It Happened One Night* (1934).

Still from 'Swimming Pool' (2003)
Ludivine Sagnier exhibits her body by the pool to attract the attention of a man (Jean-Marie Lamour) whom she wants to steal from her mother.

"When the clothed scenes are being shot, you can look out and see the director and a crew of six. Somehow, when it comes time for the bra to come off, 83 guys, including the caterer and the fellow in charge of transportation insurance, suddenly have a good and valid reason to be there."

Actress Jewel Shepard on appearing in a nude scene

Often the sexiness of a striptease is accompanied by the lure of dance and the siren call of song. In *Blonde Venus*'s campy paean to primitive desires (1932), Marlene Dietrich comes out wearing a gorilla suit, then peels it off and sings, "Hot voodoo, burn my clothes. I want to start dancing, just wearing a smile." Brigitte Bardot exudes animal sensuality in *And God Created Woman* (*Et Dieu…créa la femme*, 1956) when she runs her hands all over her body and dances the mambo in a green skirt that opens to flash her black panties. It was Bardot in this film who introduced Americans to the bikini, that sensationally revealing item of apparel which hit the country like a bomb. (Fittingly, the "bikini" got its name from a ring-shaped island in the South Pacific where nuclear weapons were tested.) In *The Wicker Man* (1973), repressed Christian Edward Woodward is driven half-crazy with desire by pagan Britt Ekland, who dances naked in the room next to his, slapping the walls and pressing up against his door in the frenzy of her lust for him.

As Michael J. Bader writes in *Arousal: The Secret Logic of Sexual Fantasies*, 'For the man, the striptease is exciting because it features a woman who is shamelessly proud of her sexuality and her body, powerfully counteracting his everyday image of women ashamed… and inhibited.' Perhaps the most guilt-free striptease is the one where Jane Fonda effortlessly defies prudes and gravity by taking off parts of her spacesuit and having them float away while she is suspended in a weightless chamber in the sex-positive comedy, *Barbarella* (1968).

Unlike female strippers, male exhibitionists are less commonly seen in film, and when they do appear, it is often in a comical context which exaggerates either their shortcomings or the extent of their prowess. Interrupted during lovemaking, super agent James Bond (Sean Connery) is proud to call attention to the fact that "you've caught me with more than my hands up" in *Diamonds Are Forever* (1971), while

BELOW
Still from 'Porky's' (1981)
Mark Herrier peers through one hole into the girls' shower room, while Wyatt Knight exposes himself through another hole.

RIGHT
Still from 'Porky's' (1981)
Kaki Hunter (far right) and the other girls in the shower room sense that they are being watched and go to investigate.

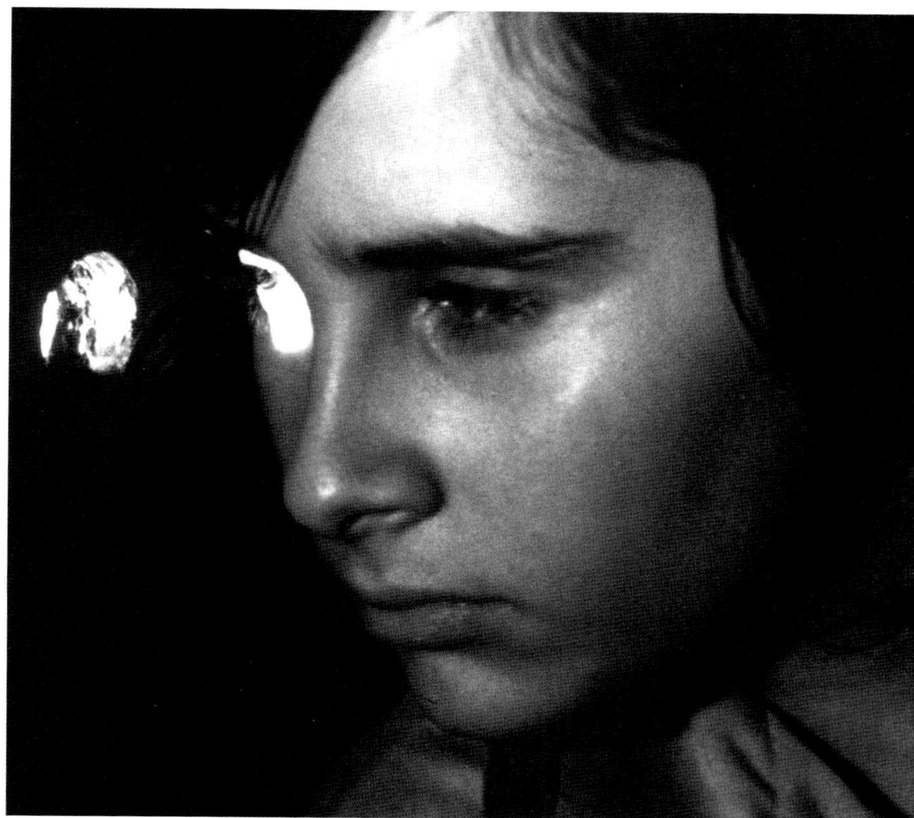

ABOVE

Still from 'The Sailor Who Fell from Grace with the Sea' (1976)

Jonathan Kahn is voyeuristic witness to his mother's self-pleasuring.

LEFT

Still from 'The Sailor Who Fell from Grace with the Sea' (1976)

Sexually desperate widow Sarah Miles caresses herself in front of the mirror.

ABOVE
Still from 'Jungle Fever' (1991)
The interracial relations between Annabella Sciorra and Wesley Snipes are already taboo, but the two increase the danger of discovery by doing it in public.

RIGHT
Still from 'The Story of Piera' (1983)
Daughter Isabelle Huppert (right) reveals her interest in committing incest with every member of her family, and her mother Hanna Schygulla seems more than willing.

OPPOSITE
Still from 'The Carpetbaggers' (1964)
Carroll Baker's striptease dance while straddling a chandelier brings the house down – in a crash of falling glass.

RIGHT
Still from 'Body Double' (1984)
Filming the campy scene where a woman taking a shower is exposed to penetration by a vampire's fangs.

BELOW
Still from 'Bull Durham' (1988)
Cocky young pitcher Tim Robbins plays ball in the (nearly) nude.

BELOW RIGHT
Still from 'A propos de Nice' (1930)
The sensual and the intellectual come together in this incongruous image from a Surrealist film: a naked woman with a book.

OPPOSITE
Still from 'The Unbearable Lightness of Being' (1988)
Lena Olin – in black lingerie and bowler hat – and Daniel Day-Lewis find that a mirror doubles their excitement.

ABOVE
Still from 'Up!' (1976)
Naked wood-nymph Kitten Natividad finds her pleasure in the wilderness.

RIGHT
Still from '9 1/2 Weeks' (1986)
Viewing erotic slides in the projection room of an art gallery prompts Kim Basinger to reach for satisfaction.

Woody Harrelson needs a ten-gallon hat to cover himself when he too is caught in the act in *The Cowboy Way* (1994). But the prize for the biggest roll-out goes to porn star Dirk Diggler (Mark Wahlberg) who unveils his incredible endowment (it is in fact a prosthesis) at the end of *Boogie Nights* (1997). By contrast, David Niven is embarrassed by the fact that his own member is only half the size of the one sculpted by his wife in *The Statue* (1971), and high-school boy Wyatt Knight finds that self-exposure can be painful when, after sticking himself through a hole in the wall of a girls' shower room in the hope of attracting their attention, he is grabbed by Balbricker, the iron-fisted gym teacher (Nancy Parsons), in *Porky's* (1981). As Peter Lehman writes in *Running Scared*, 'the sexual representation of the male body in general and the penis in particular remains a strong cultural taboo, especially in any context involving homosexuality or women looking, objectifying, assessing, talking, or desiring.'

There are, however, some remarkable instances of unabashed and unsmirking delight in male self-display. Perhaps because no one (but us) is watching, Tom Cruise seems wildly uninhibited as he slides across the floor in white socks and does a rock-'n'-roll dance in tight underwear in *Risky Business* (1983). In *To Forget Venice* (*Dimenticare Venezia*, 1979), a boy is so delighted with his own newly discovered sexuality that he walks around displaying his erection (off-screen) before the startled but admiring eyes of an entire group of washerwomen. In *Romeo and Juliet* (1968), Leonard Whiting's bare buns are the object of Olivia Hussey's (and gay director Franco Zeffirelli's) loving gaze as she wakes up in bed after a night of lovemaking to see him standing naked by the window in the morning sunlight. And in *Gimme an F* (1985), gymnast Stephen Shellen does a nearly naked high-bar routine and water-splash dance in front of two female cheerleaders, who comment that "the longer you look, the better it gets, and the better you look, the longer it gets".

Sometimes the excitement of exhibitionism comes when the most private things are made public, when they become obscene because they are seen by disapproving eyes. In *L'Age d'Or* (1930), Gaston Modot and Lya Lys get down and dirty together in the mud right in the middle of a public ceremony, while Lena Nyman and Börje Ahlstedt make politically defiant love on the lawn of the Stockholm Royal Palace in *I Am Curious (Yellow)* (*Jag Ar Nyfiken – en Film i Gult*, 1967). In *When Harry Met Sally* (1989), the diners at a deli restaurant get an earful of oral exhibitionism when Meg Ryan shrieks and moans in simulated orgasm, prompting a woman (the director's mother!) at a nearby table to tell the waiter, "I'll have what she's having."

For the voyeur, catching someone unawares in the nude or *in flagrante delicto* adds the thrill of trespass, the sense of potency that comes from invading another's privacy. Nancy Friday has written that a man's 'voyeuristic fantasies reverse the woman's power; it passes from her to the eye of the man. By keeping himself hidden or invisible, the voyeur imposes his will on the woman. She has lost her ability to say no.' An almost comically literal example of the male voyeur's omnipotence can be found in *La dolce vita* (1960) where Marcello Mastroianni is in a helicopter spying on some girls in bikinis sunbathing on a rooftop.

Illicit looking is often accompanied by another taboo practice – masturbation. Films are filled with jokes that help to discharge anxiety about masturbation while also slyly confessing pleasure in the activity. In *The Apprenticeship of Duddy Kravitz* (1974), Richard Dreyfuss tells his roommate, "Why don't you use your other hand? It might feel like having sex with someone different," while Woody Allen says, "Don't knock masturbation. It's sex with someone I love." (*Annie Hall*, 1977) To the

Still from 'Emmanuelle' (1974)
Continuing the stimulation begun by a magazine photo of Paul Newman.

"She showed me where that little button is. Now I can find that thing in the dark. And that is a good thing for a guy to know."

Brad Pitt, *Johnny Suede* (1991)

"She threw me a look I caught in my hip pocket."

Robert Mitchum, *Farewell, My Lovely* (1975)

fear that the guys who touch themselves are the lonely ones without girls to date can be added the fear/desire that masturbators are gay, as evidenced in this dialogue from *If You Don't Stop It...You'll Go Blind* (1978): "Hey, bartender, this guy's playing with himself." "So just ignore him." "I can't, he's using my hand." The fact is that men are both anxious about and proud of that big part of themselves which often makes uncontrollable demands, as can be seen from the Groucho Marx line, "One morning I shot an elephant in my pyjamas. How he got in my pyjamas, I don't know" (*Animal Crackers*, 1930), and from Mike McGlone's admission, "If I masturbated as much as I wanted to, I swear to God I would live in a constant state of guilt – not to mention hospitalization" (*The Brothers McMullen*, 1995).

In his book *Solitary Sex*, Thomas W. Laqueur gives three reasons for the negative attitudes that attached to masturbation from the early 18th century on: 'First, [masturbation] was motivated not by a real object of desire but by a phantasm [from a book or a film]. Second, while all other sex was social, masturbation was private, or, when it was not done alone, it was social in all the wrong ways [non-procreative]. And third, unlike other appetites, the urge to masturbate could be neither sated nor moderated. Done alone, driven only by the mind's own creations, it was a primal, irremediable, and seductively, even addictively, easy transgression.' At various times, masturbation was believed to cause blindness, paralysis, madness, tiredness, hair on the palms and a blot on the soul.

Despite, or because of, all these prohibitions on masturbation, movie characters have long enjoyed taking matters into their own hands and agitating against this taboo. Objects that female characters have used for self-pleasuring include a tree trunk (*Up!* 1976), a mechanical bull (*Urban Cowboy*, 1980), a flute (*The Ages of Lulu*, 1990), a spoon and some earthworms (*A Real Young Girl*, 1976), a Jacuzzi jet (*Coming Soon*, 1999), a toy scuba diver in the bath (*Tie Me Up! Tie Me Down!* 1990) and an orgasm machine (*Barbarella*, 1968). As for male characters, in *Léolo* (1992) Maxime Collin follows Alex Portnoy's lead and masturbates using a piece of liver

BELOW
Still from 'American Pie' (1999)
Horny teenager Jason Biggs is caught in a compromising position with his mother's hot apple pie.

RIGHT
Still from 'Querelle' (1982)
Jeanne Moreau complains that Brad Davis is more interested in his 'twin' brother than in her ("All you look at is yourselves; I don't exist for you"), and Davis proves her right by masturbating narcissistically.

Still from 'Murmur of the Heart' (1971)
Benoît Ferreux and his two brothers use a ruler to compare penis sizes in a scene that borders on mutual masturbation.

destined for his family's dinner, while Jason Biggs humps his mother's fresh-baked apple pie in *American Pie* (1999). To get an R rating, Biggs was not allowed to thrust too many times and he had to keep both feet on the floor, while in the unrated video version of the film he stretches out on the kitchen counter, adopting the missionary position with the pie.

Sometimes masturbation in film is more subtle and symbolic, as in *The Gang's All Here* (1943) where rows of showgirls raise and lower giant bananas, or in *The Thomas Crown Affair* (1968) when Faye Dunaway fingers the chess pieces during a match with Steve McQueen, polishing the bishop. In *L'Atalante* (1934), Jean Dasté and Dita Parlo play lovers separated by distance, and the camera cross-cuts between the two of them in their lonely beds while implying that each masturbates thinking of the other.

Unlike these wistful, romantic and humorous moments in suggestive films, movie scenes that are more explicit in their depictions of masturbation tend toward the comedy of embarrassment or the drama of something more grave. In *Fast Times at Ridgemont High* (1982), teenager Judge Reinhold masturbates in the bathroom to a slow-motion fantasy of Phoebe Cates emerging from a swimming pool and undoing her bikini top to show him her breasts – only to have Cates herself barge into the bathroom and catch him red-handed. In *There's Something About Mary* (1998), while using the toilet near a window that has a view of Cameron Diaz as she is

"Pornography is not in the hands of the child who discovers his sexuality by masturbating, but in the hands of the adult who slaps him."

Bernardo Bertolucci

changing, Ben Stiller is mistaken for a masturbating voyeur and then gets his member caught in his zipper. In a later scene, after he *has* pleasured himself, he is too embarrassed to admit it and so he watches in silence as Diaz uses his white stuff for what she thinks is hair gel. More seriously degrading is the scene in *Midnight Express* (1978) where sexually desperate Brad Davis masturbates to the sight of his girlfriend's breasts pressed up against a glass partition when she (Irene Miracle) visits him in prison. And *Ken Park* (2002) features a graphic scene of auto-erotic self-asphyxiation in which death-obsessed teenager James Ransome uses a belt tied to a doorknob to choke himself as he masturbates.

One film in which exhibitionism and voyeurism play a key part is Paul Verhoeven's *Basic Instinct* (1992), where femme fatale Catherine (Sharon Stone) flaunts her body as a way of taunting Nick (Michael Douglas), the cop who suspects her of having killed a man at the climax of S&M sex. When Nick goes to question her at her home, Catherine changes clothes in her bedroom, slyly ensuring that he catches a glimpse of her nude body. Later at a disco, Catherine does a seductive dance in a gold minidress with Roxy (Leilani Sarelle), sliding up against her lesbian friend's body and French-kissing her while Nick looks lustfully on, sidelined as a mere voyeur. But Catherine's ultimate act of exhibitionism occurs during the interrogation scene at the police station. Nick and the other detectives all have their eyes upon her as she is seated in a chair in front of them. Through a kind of eye-rape, Nick wants to penetrate Catherine's cool exterior, to have her expose her secrets to him so that he can "nail" her for the murder. But rather than give Nick the satisfaction of invading her privacy against her will, Catherine shocks Nick and the other cops by deliberately uncrossing her legs to reveal her vagina to them. (She is naked under her dress.) As Steve Rebello has said, 'Sharon Stone turned the simple act of parting her legs into the screen's greatest special effect since Charlton Heston parted the Red Sea in *The Ten Commandments*.' By flaunting her female sexuality, Catherine overpowers her onlookers and causes the cops to wilt from embarrassment.

"I can never get a zipper to close. Maybe that stands for something. What do you think?"

Rita Hayworth, *Gilda* (1946)

BELOW LEFT
Still from 'Basic Instinct' (1992)
Police investigators think that they have Catherine (Sharon Stone) in the hot seat as they bear down upon her with their interrogation.

BELOW RIGHT
Still from 'Basic Instinct' (1992)
The police themselves are suddenly made to sweat when Catherine (Sharon Stone) coolly uncrosses her legs and flashes her sex at them, recalling the ancient belief in the power of the exposed vagina to repel foes or expel demons.

OPPOSITE
Still from 'Basic Instinct' (1992)
Though Michael Douglas's contract contained a 'penis clause' prohibiting his genitals from being shown, he does bare his bulging torso in this scene with Sharon Stone.

Fellatio / Cunnilingus / Sodomy

In *The Postman Always Rings Twice* (1946), a tube of lipstick rolls across the floor and comes to rest at a man's feet. John Garfield picks it up and hands it to Lana Turner, who uses it to rouge her lips, outlining the mouth as an erogenous zone. Some people are said to believe that a woman's mouth and lips indicate the size and shape of her vagina. Silent-film star Clara Bow had 'cupid-bow' lips. Marilyn Monroe and Brigitte Bardot had 'bee-stung' lips, pursed and pouty, while Angelina Jolie and Béatrice Dalle's lips are famously full and tumid. Photographer Cecil Beaton once described Joan Crawford's lips as having 'the colour and splash and latitude of a split persimmon. This labial flamboyancy is her most arresting feature.'

Sometimes all lips have to do is talk to be sexy. In *Before Sunrise* (1995), Julie Delpy and Ethan Hawke spend an entire night engaged in intimate conversation while wandering around Vienna, and in *Lost in Translation* (2003) Bill Murray and Scarlett Johansson have become soul mates by the time they fall asleep in a Tokyo hotel bed, fully clothed and barely touching, after talking all night. *Bent* (1996) has Clive Owen and Lothaire Bluteau as homosexual lovers in a Nazi concentration camp who are prohibited from touching, but we see them walking side by side and bringing each other to orgasm solely by word of mouth.

Ever since the advent of talking pictures, audiences have thrilled to the seductive voices of movie stars. 'GARBO TALKS!' proclaimed the ads for *Anna Christie* (1930), and she certainly did, playing a prostitute who enters a bar and says in her deep husky voice, "Give me a whiskey, ginger ale on the side, and don't be stingy, baby." By contrast, in *His Glorious Night* (1929), the coming of sound hastened the end of screen lover John Gilbert's career when his "I love you, I love you" provoked laughter due to his dainty and high-pitched voice. Female stars known for their enticing talk include the smoky-voiced Lauren Bacall, who tells Humphrey Bogart, "You know how to whistle, don't you? You just put your lips together and blow." (*To Have and Have Not*, 1944) In *Body Heat* (1981), sultry-sounding Kathleen Turner nabs William Hurt with her brazen pick-up line, "You aren't too bright. I like that in a man." Turner also provides the come-hither voice for naughty cartoon bunny Jessica Rabbit ("I'm not bad. I'm just drawn that way") in *Who Framed Roger Rabbit?* (1988). Perhaps most notable of all is the honeyed and husky voice of Marilyn Monroe, whose kiss-kiss mouth whispers and purrs to Tom Ewell in *The Seven Year Itch* (1955), "When it gets hot like this, you know what I do? I keep my

Still from 'Talk to Her' (2002)
In an imaginary film-within-the-film, 'The Shrinking Man' (Fele Martínez) seeks love and comfort inside his girlfriend's sex.

'The clitoris is the most sensitive, nerve-filled part of a woman's body. The glans alone harbours over 8,000 nerve fibres (twice *the number found in the penis).'*

Terri Hamilton, ***Skin Flutes & Velvet Gloves***

LEFT
Still from 'I'm No Angel' (1933)
Mae West sashays, shimmies, and sings 'Sister Honky-Tonk', showing that "I used to be Snow White, but I drifted." West raised sexual innuendo to the level of an art form, and her wit is still unsurpassed.

RIGHT TOP
Still from 'Get Carter' (1971)
Britt Ekland is being told to put her hand down her panties by Michael Caine on the other end of the line in this phone sex scene.

RIGHT
Still from 'Tokyo Decadence' (1992)
A prostitute sings a song, karaoke style, using a vibrating dildo as a microphone.

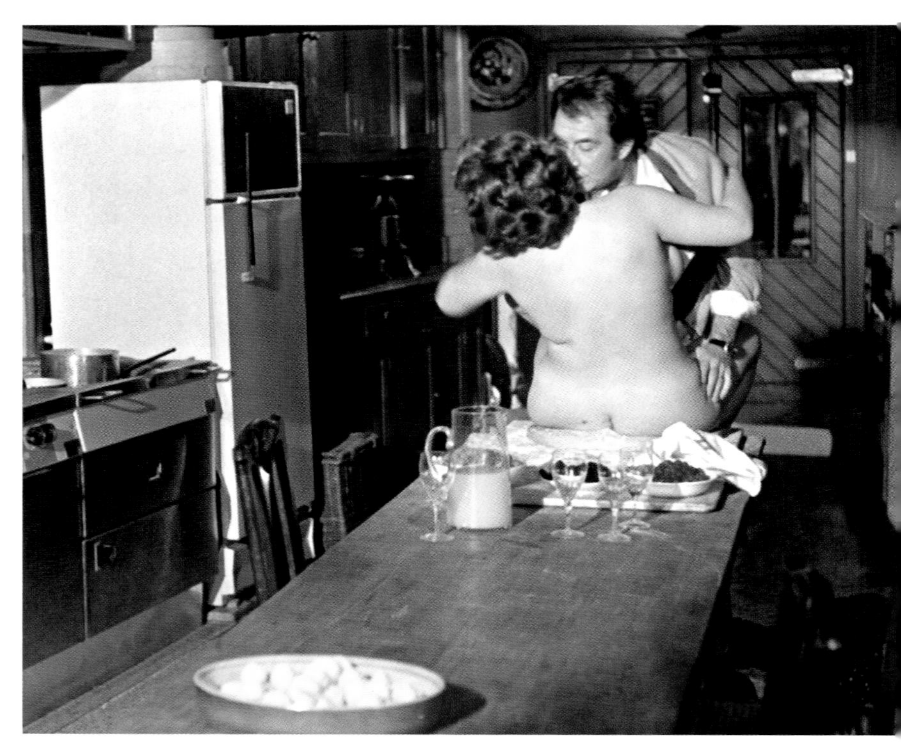

RIGHT
Still from 'La Grande Bouffe' (1973)
Ugo Tognazzi feasts on the flesh of Florence Giorgetti as part of his plan to die from overindulgence in food and sex.

BELOW
Still from 'The Cook, the Thief, His Wife & Her Lover' (1989)
Helen Mirren and Alan Howard find that their carnal appetites are whetted by the meats and cheeses in a restaurant pantry.

Still from 'Tom Jones' (1963)
Albert Finney and Joyce Redman hungrily devour their meat and drink in what some consider to be the most erotic eating scene in movie history.

undies in the icebox." Billy Wilder once remarked that "No one ever sounded as blonde as Marilyn Monroe did." Oddly, Clint Eastwood is said to have developed the heavy pauses in his tough-guy way of talking by studying Monroe's breathy speech patterns.

The first film actress to become a sensation for her sex talk was Mae West, whose shameless one-liners resound through history as provocative evidence of female desire: "When I'm good, I'm very good, but when I'm bad, I'm better" (*I'm No Angel*, 1933); "When women go wrong, men go right after them" (*She Done Him Wrong*, 1933). While Mae West's bawdy wisecracks may seem funny to us, they were no laughing matter to the Catholic Legion of Decency, whose protests led Hollywood to censor itself by creating the Production Code.

As suggested by one of her notorious lines – "I've been on more laps than a napkin" (*I'm No Angel*) – the full-figured, big-breasted West was not shy about confessing her sexual appetites. Indeed, food and sex often go together in film, pointing up another connection between the oral and the erotic. Grace Kelly is offering more than cold chicken to Cary Grant when she asks him, "Do you want a leg or a breast?" while on a picnic in *To Catch a Thief* (1955). In *Tom Jones* (1963), Joyce Redman and Albert Finney devour a roast chicken with finger-licking delectation, and Jennifer Beals sucks lobster out of its shell while talking dirty to Michael Nouri at a seafood restaurant in *Flashdance* (1983). Most memorably, in *9 1/2 Weeks* (1986), Mickey Rourke blindfolds a naked Kim Basinger and then feeds her an olive, maraschino cherries, a cherry tomato, strawberries, champagne, cough syrup, spiral pasta, cherry Jello, jalapeño peppers, milk, sparkling water and honey.

Rourke also melts ice cubes on Basinger's breasts. Freud considered the breast to be the first erogenous zone. The pleasure of suckling is the oral phase of a child's sexual development, to be followed by the anal and genital stages. In *The Girl Can't*

'According to scientific research, the nutritional value of a tablespoon of semen is equal to that of two pieces of New York steak, ten eggs, six oranges, and two lemons – combined.'

Terri Hamilton, ***Skin Flutes & Velvet Gloves***

Help It (1956), when he sees Jayne Mansfield carrying two milk bottles pressed against her 42DD breasts, a milkman's own bottle pops its cap and overflows. *The Sign of the Cross* (1932) also appeals to erotic infantile longings for the breast in the scene where Claudette Colbert bathes naked in a tub of asses' milk, her breasts bobbing on the surface. Some breasts are good enough to eat, like Penélope Cruz's, which taste like ham to her lover Javier Bardem who licks them in *Jamón, Jamón* (1992). The connection among food, breasts and sex can be seen in Eve's apple-like breasts, which are associated with the apple of the Fall.

Eden also has its phallic snake which is supposed to have seduced Eve into sin. Like suckling at the breast, sucking penile objects can satisfy longings for infantile oral gratification. When child-woman Carroll Baker sucks her thumb or licks an ice cream cone in *Baby Doll* (1956), and when nymphet Sue Lyon licks a lollipop or sucks Coca-Cola through a straw in *Lolita* (1962), they are half-way between mother and lover, breast-feeding and fellatio. *Fast Times at Ridgemont High* (1982) has Phoebe Cates teaching Jennifer Jason Leigh a lesson in oral sex using a carrot in a high school lunchroom, while in *Celebrity* (1998) Bebe Neuwirth hands Judy Davis a banana and says, "Give me your best blow job."

The excitement of some fellatio scenes comes from defying prudish authorities, as in *Shampoo* (1975) when Julie Christie crawls under the table at a political fundraiser to perform oral sex on Warren Beatty, while televisions in the background show a politician denouncing permissiveness. Other fellatio scenes get their sexual charge from the sadomasochistic power play between the two participants. In *Carnal Knowledge* (1971), Jack Nicholson has to pay prostitute Rita Moreno to enlarge his ego by submitting orally to him ("you're getting hard – more strong, more masculine – it's rising – more virile, more domineering – it's up!"), and David Wissak almost drowns Katia Golubeva by forcing her head to stay down on him in a swimming pool in *Twentynine Palms* (2003). But even though it is the woman who goes down on the man, this does not mean that she is necessarily subservient to him. *Disclosure* (1994) has Demi Moore kneeling down to unzip the pants on employee Michael Douglas while instructing him to "just lie back and let me be the boss", and Jennifer Jason Leigh uses her oral skills to seduce the boyfriend of her female rival in *Single White Female* (1992). As Alan Soble has pointed out, the power balance in fellatio is by no means self-evident: 'we can see the woman eagerly performing fellatio as submissively subservient to the man's desire, or as a sluttish glutton for her own pleasure, or as a woman enjoying sex without making excuses.'

Certainly, fellatio has been a staple of pornographic movies, figuring most prominently in the first mainstream hardcore hit, *Deep Throat* (1972), where Linda Lovelace plays a woman who discovers that her clitoris is located in her throat and that fellatio is the only way for her to reach orgasm. Recently, some art films have blurred the line between pornography and mainstream cinema by depicting unsimulated fellatio, including *Romance* (1999), *Intimacy* (2000) and *9 Songs* (2004). Some accused actor/director Vincent Gallo of narcissism for having Chloë Sevigny perform oral sex on him in his film, *The Brown Bunny* (2003), and for advertising the movie with a billboard on Sunset Boulevard featuring a giant (blurred) image of the fellatio scene.

In the history of film, cunnilingus has been less commonly seen than fellatio. Male fears and desires regarding the female sex are sometimes expressed through fanciful depictions of cunnilingus. The horror comedy *Re-Animator* (1984) deals with castration anxiety in the scene where a decapitated man 'gives head' to a

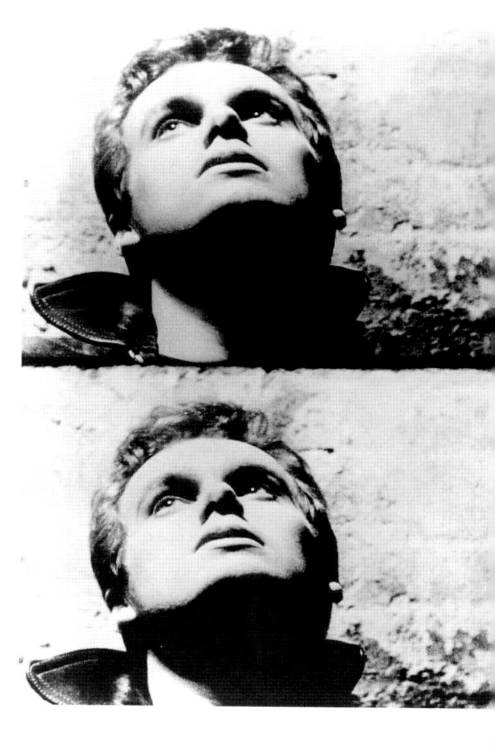

ABOVE
Still from 'Blow Job' (1963)
The camera holds on Tom Baker's face and its changing expressions while someone is busy below the waist (off-screen) in Andy Warhol's underground classic.

OPPOSITE TOP
Still from 'Color of Night' (1994)
Bruce Willis was brave enough not to use a body double for this scene where, in the unrated version, he is fully exposed as Jane March goes down on him underwater.

OPPOSITE BOTTOM LEFT
Still from 'P.O. Box Tinto Brass' (1995)
A fellatio fantasy is acted out in this film by director Tinto Brass based on salacious letters he has received from female fans.

OPPOSITE BOTTOM RIGHT
Still from 'La Grande Bouffe' (1973)
Florence Giorgetti gorges herself on Philippe Noiret in this film about sexual gluttons.

ABOVE
Still from 'In the Realm of Passion' (1978)
Tatsuya Fuji claims Kazuko Yoshiyuki's body as his own by tonguing her sex, shaving her pubic hair and then strangling her husband.

RIGHT
Still from 'Color of Night' (1994)
Underwater diving is one of the adventures in this erotic thriller, starring Jane March and Bruce Willis.

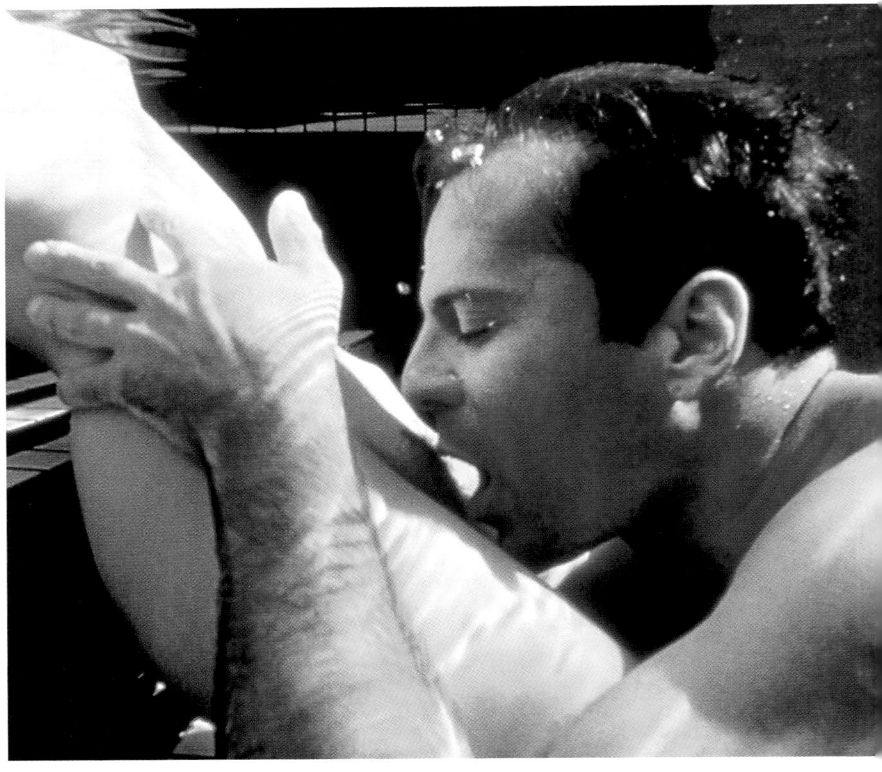

Susan Sarandon: "But why would one of his women want to kill him?"
Judith Ivey: "Maybe he wouldn't go down on her."
Susan Sarandon: "Don't you think murder is just a little bit excessive?"
Judith Ivey: "I most certainly do not."

Compromising Positions **(1985)**

woman, while *Talk to Her* (2002) evinces a longing to return to the womb in its fantasy of a miniaturized man who finds safety by crawling into his girlfriend's vagina. Implied cunnilingus can slip under the censor's radar. There is suggested oral sex in *Romancing the Stone* (1984) when, after they tumble together down a hill in a mudslide, Michael Douglas lands head-first in Kathleen Turner's lap. The cunnilingual implications of the notorious shot in *The Graduate* (1967) where virginal Dustin Hoffman's face is framed inside Anne Bancroft's leg are made explicit in *Ken Park* (2002), with its lingering shot of teenage James Bullard licking between the legs of his girlfriend's mother, Maeve Quinlan. Big-name stars fed their carnal appetites in the 1990s, with Michael Douglas performing oral sex with considerable enthusiasm on Sharon Stone in *Basic Instinct* (1992), and Bruce Willis taking the plunge by going down on Jane March in a swimming pool in *Color of Night* (1994). More recently, *In the Cut* (2003) has Meg Ryan shed her goody-two-shoes image along with her clothes when Mark Ruffalo takes her to bed, plants her on her stomach, spreads her legs, and eats her out from behind, prompting her to ask, "Who taught you *that?*" And then there's the moment in *Gigli* (2003) when Jennifer Lopez spreads her own legs and tells Ben Affleck, "It's turkey time – gobble gobble!"

If cunnilingus and fellatio return us to the infantile oral delights of sucking and eating, then sodomy may take us back to the sphincteral pleasures of the anal stage in our childhood sexual development. Since religious moralists have worked hard to make us feel guilty about our sex organs and bodily functions, oral and anal sex may seem dirty or disgusting, but this also gives them a considerable transgressive charge, a sense that to engage in them is to break deep and longstanding taboos. As Alan Soble has written, 'The anus, mouth, and genitalia can be both beautiful and disgusting, and maybe their appeal is, like sweet-and-sour Chinese, exactly that biting or burning combination.'

In some films, the excitement of anal sex comes from cruelty and degradation, from breaking bodies and rules. Defiling the sanctity of marriage with non-procreative sex, fascists sodomize a couple of newlyweds in *Salo, or The 120 Days of Sodom* (*Salò, o le 120 giornate de Sodoma*, 1976). In *Storytelling* (2001), white female student Selma Blair is placed with her face against a wall and taken anally by black teacher Robert Wilson, who completes his defiance of the ban on interracial sex by making her say, "Nigger, fuck me hard." More subtle but still devastating in an emotional sense is the scene in *Fat Girl* (*A ma soeur*, 2001) where lustful older student Libero de Rienzo sweet-talks young Roxane Mesquida into painful sodomy by saying that she'll do it for him if she loves him and that anal sex isn't really sex because she gets to keep her virginity. By contrast, other films show that sodomy can be pleasurable for the receptive partner as well, though this may be a pleasure that grows out of pain. In *Querelle* (1982), sailor Brad Davis winces but eventually enjoys being taken from behind by macho brothel-owner Günther Kaufmann, and Jane Birkin's cries of pain become moans of pleasure when Joe Dallesandro sodomizes her in the back of a garbage truck in *Je t'aime moi non plus* (1976).

Still from 'Kama Sutra: A Tale of Love' (1996)
Lesbian cunnilingus is among the many varied acts and positions demonstrated as love lessons ('Kama Sutra') in this movie.

PAGE 110
Still from 'Arabian Nights' (1974)
Prince Tagi (Francesco Paolo Governale) and Princess Dunya (Abadit Ghidei) celebrate sex as both a ceremonial ritual and a natural appetite. This scene is more revealing because of what it fails at concealing.

PAGE 111
Still from 'Shampoo' (1975)
Hairdresser Warren Beatty gives such good blow jobs that he gets them from women in return.

Still from 'Last Tango in Paris' (1972)
Lovers Jeanne (Maria Schneider) and Paul (Marlon Brando) sit entwined. Norman Mailer wanted the sex scenes to be even more explicit: 'Brando's real cock up Schneider's real vagina would have brought the history of film one huge march closer to the ultimate experience.'

The most famous act of sodomy on film is the "Go get the butter" scene from Bernardo Bertolucci's *Last Tango in Paris* (1972), where Paul (Marlon Brando) pins Jeanne (Maria Schneider) face down on the floor, uses butter as a lubricant, and then takes her anally. One meaning of this act is that it is unlike the missionary position where lovers enjoy the intimacy of looking each other in the face. Paul has insisted that when he and Jeanne meet daily in an empty Paris apartment, they are to know nothing about each other, not even their names, and sodomy drives home this sense of impersonality. But despite Paul's desire for pure sex uncomplicated by identities or lives outside that apartment, his buggering of Jeanne is really an act of displaced anger at his wife, whom he blames for having abandoned him by sleeping with another man and then by committing suicide. Paul vents his anger in sexual aggression against Jeanne, degrading her because he can no longer take revenge on his wife. In addition, Paul uses sodomy to defile the bourgeois ideal of marriage, which he feels that his wife betrayed when she was unfaithful to him. If married sex is procreative, leading to future generations, anal sex leads nowhere, and when Paul buggers Jeanne, he forces her to speak a denunciation of marriage and family as false ideals. Later, Paul orders her to cut her nails and then stick her fingers up his rectum, telling her that she must "go right up into the ass of death" to conquer her fear of loneliness. Paul had thought that his wife would be with him until death do they part, and it is his own fear of having been left to die alone that he is trying to conquer by facing the absolute worst, which to him means being sodomized.

Still from 'Last Tango in Paris' (1972)
Strangers Jeanne and Paul come together violently for anonymous sex and then roll apart, with Schneider revealing a much-discussed flash of pubic hair.

'What seems nasty, painful, evil, can become a source of beauty, joy, and strength, if faced with an open mind.'

Writer Henry Miller on anal sex

Still from 'Last Tango in Paris' (1972)
A tender moment between Paul and Jeanne – unlike the violent sodomy scene involving butter. After that scene, said Brando, "waiters in restaurants would bring me butter with a funny smile."

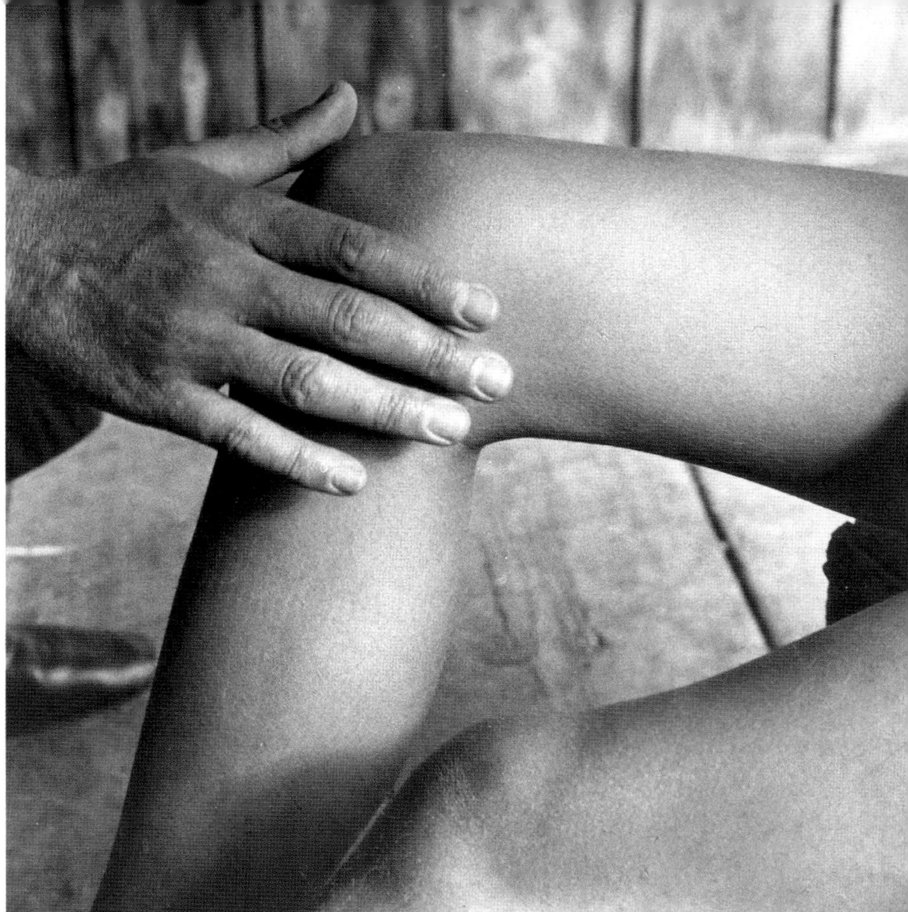

Gere, but straight hair right after they have had sex. The startling change is probably just a continuity error, but many were amused to read it as a sign of how good it had been for her. At the opposite extreme, in the futuristic society of THX 1138 (1971) where love is forbidden, all heads must be kept shaved.

As for hair down there, it is implied by the velvet pants worn by Greta Garbo in *Queen Christina* (1933) and the patch of velvet stroked by Dennis Hopper in *Blue Velvet* (1986). It is strongly suggested by Marlene Dietrich's fur cape in *The Scarlet Empress* (1934) and the shag carpet on which Brigitte Bardot lies in *Contempt* (*Le Mépris*, 1963). And it is virtually made explicit by the animal-skin bikini on cavewoman Raquel Welch in *One Million Years B.C.* (1966). *Blow-Up* (1966) was the first mainstream film to show flashes of actual pubic hair, in a scene where would-be models Jane Birkin and Gillian Hills wrestle with photographer David Hemmings on some purple backdrop paper, whereas in *Dressed to Kill* (1980) the pubic hair on Angie Dickinson's body double had to be air-brushed out during the shower rape fantasy for the film to get an R rating. Speaking about this kind of censorship, director Ken Russell has said, "That's very unfortunate because if we take out all the pubic hair, there won't be much left to the movies, will there?" Certainly, Julianne Moore is one performer who has shown courage in this regard. When she performs an extended dramatic scene in *Short Cuts* (1994) after taking off the skirt she spilled wine on, our surprise comes from seeing an actress of Moore's calibre standing there in her red pubes. It is this lower region of Carole Bouquet that Fernando Rey keeps trying but failing to see in *That Obscure Object of Desire* (*Cet obscur objet du désir*,

Fetishes

Page 120 Top Left: 'Capriccio' (1987) Foot-kissing is a metaphor for fellatio in this film about erotic escapades on the island of Capri.
Page 120 Bottom Left: 'One Night at McCool's' (2001) Femme fatale Liv Tyler zeroes in on Paul Reiser's ear as an erogenous zone.
Page 120 Centre Top: 'Venus in Furs' (1969) Dennis Price strokes and kisses a leg in submissive devotion to fur-clad dominatrix Maria Rohm. She goes on to captivate and kill him by striking a number of sensuous but deadly poses in a mirror.
Page 120 Centre Bottom: 'The Balcony' (1963) Judge Peter Brocco prostrates himself before the high-heeled shoes of Ruby Dee in this film based on a Jean Genet play.
Page 121 Top Right: 'Dreams That Money Can Buy' (1947) A female mannequin is set up to begin a romance with another store-window dummy in the 'Girl with the Prefabricated Heart' segment of this Surrealist dream film.
Page 121 Bottom Right: 'The Sexual Life of the Belgians' (1994) Flemish anarchist Jan Bucquoy finds pneumatic bliss with a sex doll at the end of his seriocomic quest for erotic fulfilment.

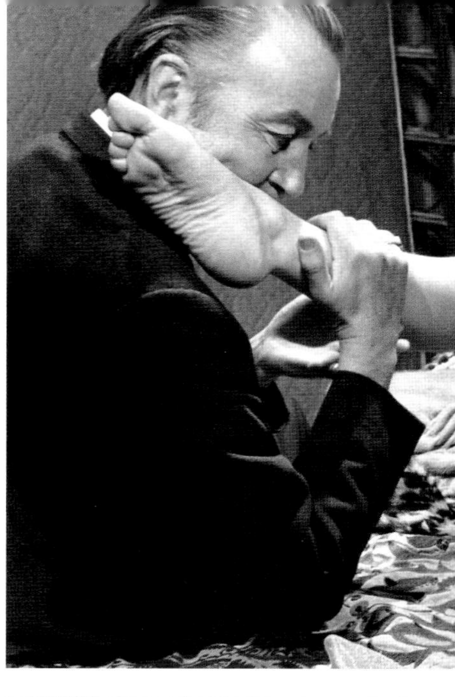

Fetishes

Top Left: 'Capriccio' (1987)
Left: 'One Night at McCool's' (2001)
Centre Top: 'Venus in Furs' (1969)

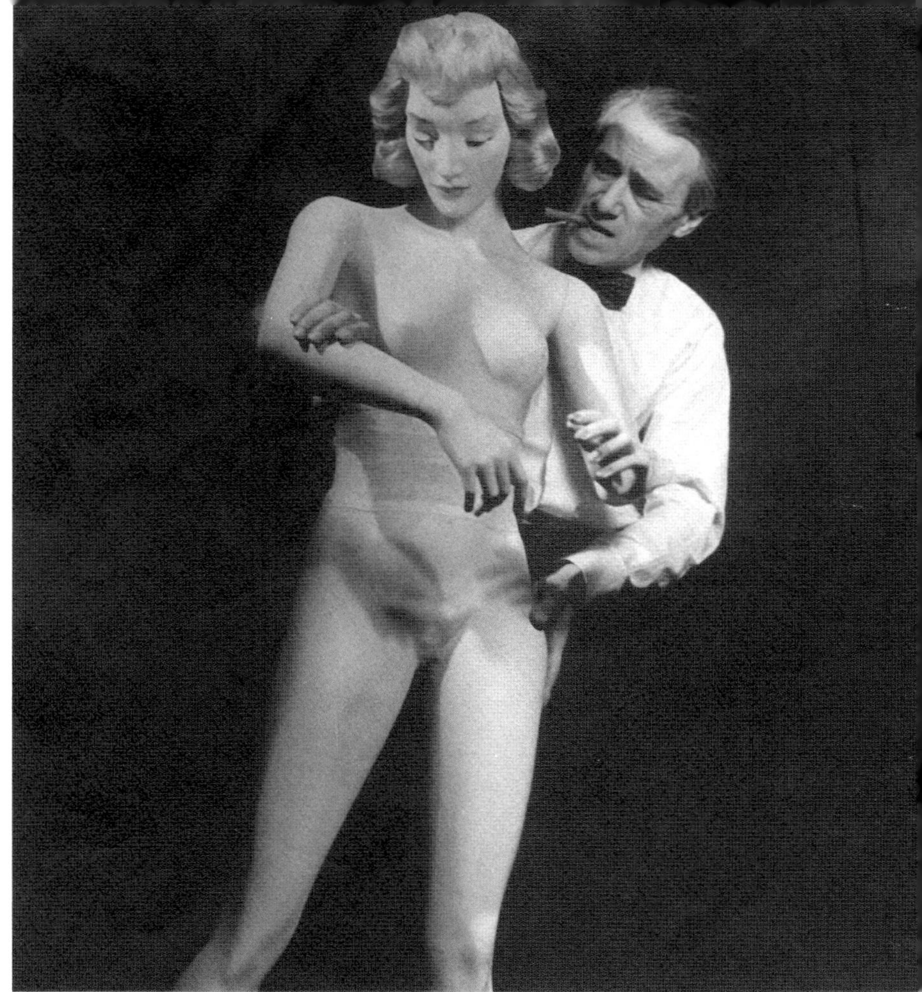

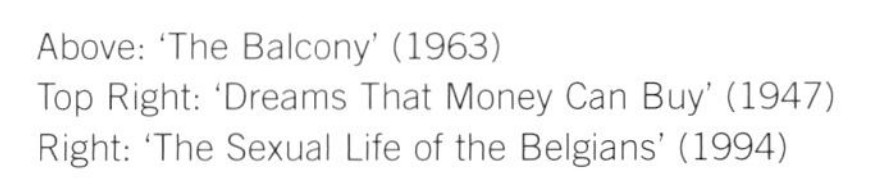

Above: 'The Balcony' (1963)
Top Right: 'Dreams That Money Can Buy' (1947)
Right: 'The Sexual Life of the Belgians' (1994)

ABOVE
Still from 'Un Chien Andalou' (1928)
In the next shot, these fondled breasts will dissolve into cupped buttocks, as a man appreciates the rounded shapes of a woman in this Surrealist film by Luis Buñuel and Salvador Dalí.

RIGHT
Still from 'I Spit on Your Grave' (1959)
Christian Marquand plays a light-skinned black man who avenges the lynching of his brother by going after white women – in this case, with a shower nozzle – in this rare film noir. The water highlights her heaving breasts.

1977). When he finally gets her into bed, he discovers that under her nightgown she is wearing an elaborately laced corset which impedes his progress as effectively as a chastity belt. The corset is itself a powerful fetish, calling attention to what it conceals, inciting while also thwarting desire – 'a neat package of sexual allure and moral rectitude tied up with pink ribbons', as Judith Thurman puts it. And speaking of things hidden, the innermost secret of "Rosebud" in *Citizen Kane* (1941) is not that it was a sled, but that reputedly it was William Randolph Hearst's pet name for the clitoris of his mistress Marion Davies. Words can be fetishes, too.

There is also a long history of phallic fetishes on film – objects that suggest or substitute for the male sexual organ. The most blatant of these is the vibrator. Interestingly, vibrators were advertised in the early 1900s as home appliances that could improve health, induce relaxation and polish the furniture. A 1918 ad in the Sears Roebuck catalogue featured vibrators as 'Aids That Every Woman Appreciates'. However, when 1930s stag films showed that vibrators were being used as dildos, these handy gadgets disappeared from household shopping catalogues. Male anxiety may have been one reason for this disappearance. An example of what can happen occurs in *9 Songs* (2004) when Margo Stilley ends up being more interested in her vibrator than in her boyfriend Kieran O'Brian. Phallic imagery in mainstream films is usually somewhat less direct than a vibrating dildo, and it can turn up in the most unlikely places. Controversy erupted over the film poster for *The Little Mermaid* (1989) because one of the castle towers looks like a male erection, while in another children's film, *The Cat in the Hat* (2003), a mother's portrait opens into a centrefold, which gets a rise out of the Cat's hat. In *The Mask of Zorro* (1998), Antonio Banderas' sword springs up at the sight of a slashed opening in Catherine Zeta-Jones' dress which he has just made with his blade, and in *Mo' Better Blues* (1990) musician Denzel Washington trumpets his interest in Cynda Williams' body as she undresses in front of him. Phallic fulfilment seems easy and all-natural in *Liane, Jungle Goddess* (*Liane, das Mädchen aus dem Urwald*, 1956) when Marion Michael wraps her legs around the trunk of a tree and climbs it, whereas size and potency would seem to be the point of naked Gilda Texter astride a roaring motorcycle in *Vanishing Point* (1971). Penile eroticism gets creepy when pimp Harvey Keitel slow-dances with child prostitute Jodie Foster, running his hands with their cocaine-scooping pinkie-nail all over her in *Taxi Driver* (1976), and when vampire Klaus Kinski lifts up Isabelle Adjani's skirt with his long and long-dead fingernails in *Nosferatu* (1979).

The idea of phallic fetishes potent with danger can lead us into the area of perversion known as bestiality. Here the fantasy is one of being taken by a sexual animal, a primitive brute who will forcibly awaken the desires that civilization has renounced and repressed. In *The Beast* (*La Bête*, 1974), aristocratic Sirpa Lane is chased through the woods by a hairy priapic creature, stripped of her lace garments and her inhibitions, and opened up to prolonged pleasure. As Marjorie Garber explains in *Dog Love*, 'the appeal/repulsion of bestiality' lies in 'the experience of crossing a forbidden line – taking the pleasures of the body past repression, past morality, even past humanity'. The sexual pairings of woman and animal on film are as varied as the human imagination, including relations with a chimpanzee (*Max mon amour*, 1986), a German shepherd (*491*, 1964), a horse (*Emmanuelle in America*, 1976), a zebra (*A Zed & Two Noughts*, 1985), a pig (*8 1/2 Women*, 1999), a bull (*Why?* 1973) and a ménage à trois with a poodle (*Caniche*, 1979). Of course,

"I see Dracula as not even existing. He's just a big, pleasurable lust fluttering around from woman to woman."

Guy Maddin, director of *Dracula: Pages from a Virgin's Diary* (2002)

BELOW
Still from 'Dracula' (1931)
Vampire Bela Lugosi is about to penetrate Helen Chandler's neck. "Ah, what letters women wrote me," said Lugosi, "letters of a horrible hunger, asking if I cared only for maiden's blood!"

LEFT
Still from 'The Criminal Life of Archibaldo de la Cruz' (1955)
Ernesto Alonso and Miroslava Stern play a teasing game with a dummy double of her. When he makes sexual advances to the dummy, she reprimands him for going too far.

women can be beasts in the bedroom too, as when panther-woman Kathleen Burke claws the back of her lover in *The Island of Lost Souls* (1933), or when lady-turned-leopard Nastassja Kinski rubs her feral face on Malcolm McDowell's neck and then later has to be tied to the bedposts by her lover John Heard, who is afraid that her ravenous desires will get out of control during sex in *Cat People* (1982).

Another kind of film that tries to imagine animal passion unfettered by civilized restraint or religious censure is the pagan genre. But there is no going back to the Garden of Eden, and attempts to picture Adam and Eve in the nude without shame or having sex without guilt always meet with cries of indecency and calls for censorship. In *Tarzan and His Mate* (1934), Johnny Weissmuller grabs Maureen O'Sullivan and playfully tosses her into a lagoon, ripping her jungle dress off in midair, but the embarrassed censors cut this scene along with the entirety of her nude swim that followed. And for good measure, they insisted that O'Sullivan's jungle dress cover more of her breasts and that Weissmuller's loincloth be lengthened by several inches. It seems that natural nudity can only bring down the wrath of the censor or excite prurient interest, as in Groucho Marx's sniggering comment in *Animal Crackers* (1930): "We took some pictures of the native girls, but they weren't developed. We're going back in a few weeks." In *And God Created Woman* (*Et Dieu…créa la femme*, 1956), Brigitte Bardot's amoral indulgence of her sex drive with multiple men led feminist Simone de Beauvoir to praise her – 'She eats when she is hungry and she makes love in the same matter-of-fact manner' – but it also led to her being "condemned from more pulpits than Satan", as Bardot herself noted. When sex symbol Mae West made a film called *It Ain't No Sin* (1933), Catholic ministers picketed theatres, carrying signs that read, "IT IS". Perhaps the most powerful defence of female sensuality as beyond good and evil is what Marcello Mastroianni says to Anita Ekberg as they dance together in *La dolce vita* (1960): "You are the first woman on the first day of creation. You are mother, sister, lover, friend, angel, devil, earth, home."

Some films find erotic excitement in the friction between religious repression and pagan desires. In *Black Narcissus* (1946), a group of nuns in the Himalayan Mountains struggles to remain chaste, even though their convent was a former harem, sensual murals still decorate the walls and native drumbeats throb at night. *Behind Convent Walls* (*Interno di un convento*, 1977) shows us one love-starved nun using a dildo whose handle is engraved with the face of Jesus Christ, while *Immagini di un Convento* (1979) has a nun in a white nightgown and black stockings masturbate drowsily in her bed and then be fondled in her sleep by another nun. These moments of secretive pleasuring get an extra erotic charge out of guilt, fear of punishment and the blasphemous use of religious artefacts for sensual ends.

Repressed desires really break out in *The Devils* (1971) in a scene where a whole convent of medieval nuns exhibits mass sexual hysteria. After tearing off their habits, the naked nuns pull a statue of Christ down from a wall, straddle it, and have sex on its face, torso, and genital area, while a priest who is watching masturbates under his cassock. It is not clear whether the nuns are really hysterical or are merely performing the acts required of them by a witch-hunting Inquisitor, who has threatened them with death if they do not show signs of possession by the devil. Witches were expected to reveal a third breast from which the devil sucked blood as nourishment, and witches' confessions were supposed to give detailed descriptions of the devil's enormous organ and its entrance into their vaginas, which were considered the gates of hell. Thus, Church Inquisitors in their fear of sexuality were

"I was promised 'tasteful nudity', which in this case meant that I got to be topless in front of the Eiffel Tower. We shot it when there were no gendarmes about, on a dreary morning with the temperature hovering around eight degrees… and that's Fahrenheit. All I can recall is that my nipples looked like the pop-up timers on Butterball turkeys, and there were tourists taking photos and muttering, 'Now this is what Paris should be like.'"

Actress Jewel Shepard

ABOVE
Still from 'Gothic' (1986)
Percy Shelley (Julian Sands) has an erotic nightmare of his sister Claire (Myriam Cyr) revealing that she has breasts with eyes.

OPPOSITE
Stills from 'Mahler' (1974)
A fantasy sequence where Jewish composer Gustav Mahler (Robert Powell, depicted in the painting) imagines himself being forced to convert to Aryan Christianity, which he associates with a Nazi transvestite dominatrix who gets him to perform sexual perversions in submission to her.

ABOVE

Still from 'The Canterbury Tales' (1972)

A Charlie Chaplin-like innocent (Ninetto Davoli) suddenly gets a whole lot of experience in the form of dancing naked women, some of whom wear hats that look sacrilegiously like nun's wimples.

LEFT

Still from 'Black Narcissus' (1946)

Sister Clodagh (Deborah Kerr, on the right) is shocked to see that Sister Ruth (Kathleen Byron) has removed her nun's habit and put on a red dress and lipstick to go out into the night in search of a man.

OPPOSITE

Still from 'Behind Convent Walls' (1977)

Erotic friction results from combining two things that we don't normally see together: 'masturbating' and 'nun.'

ABOVE

Still from 'The Last Temptation of Christ' (1988)

Christ (Willem Dafoe) must resist the temptation of a normal life, which includes the loving attention of family and friends as well as the erotic attentions of Mary Magdalene, with whom he imagines making love in a later scene that some protested as blasphemous.

TOP RIGHT

Still from 'Crimes of Passion' (1984)

Anthony Perkins plays a hypocritical preacher whose fiery sermons against prostitutes are fuelled by his own burning desires.

RIGHT

Still from 'Häxan (Witchcraft Through the Ages' (1922)

A monk tries to save a nun – and himself – from giving in to devilish temptations of the flesh in this sensationalistic Swedish film about witchcraft.

Still from 'Crash' (1996)
Catherine (Deborah Kara Unger) is thrown from her car when James rear-ends it off the road. "She starts to cry because she really doesn't want to be all right; she wants more, more of a crash, closer to death," director David Cronenberg explains.

'Eroticism, it may be said, is assenting to life up to the point of death.'

Georges Bataille, *Erotism: Death & Sensuality*

Sadomasochism / Rape

In *Goin' to Town* (1935), when Paul Cavanagh says to Mae West, "You're a dangerous woman," her reply is, "Thanks. You look good to me, too." Erotic force that overrides another's resistance, the swoon of succumbing to unbearable delights – even early films are rife with sadomasochistic implications such as these. In *The Beast of the City* (1932), Wallace Ford tells Jean Harlow that she had better behave herself or he will beat her up and she wouldn't like that. Her response is, "Oh, I don't know, depends if it's done in the right sort of way." "Take it and like it!" is what Clark Gable says as he shoves Norma Shearer back onto a couch in *A Free Soul* (1931) – a push so violent that many viewers incorrectly remember it as a punch – while in *Red-Headed Woman* (1932) Chester Morris slaps Jean Harlow across the face, to which she replies, "Do it again! I like it!" To these early examples of female masochism can be added one of sadism in the iconic image of Marlene Dietrich as *The Scarlet Empress* (1934), accessorized with sensuous white fur, man-crushing boots and a delightfully stinging whip.

For many people, pain is the opposite of pleasure, and rape is as far from romance as you can get. To see film violence as erotic may seem like condoning it in real life. However, as feminist Lynne Segal argues, 'We are all… entitled to a lowering of ignorance about the nature and force of fantasy, and hence to the lowering of personal anxiety about the sources of sexual excitement. Pornographic fantasy has no straightforward connection with what would be presumed to be its "real-life" enactment.' Like our dreams, film can be a safe place for the exploration of dangerous sexual fantasies, for the fulfilment of desires that could cause damage or even death in the real world.

In *Belle de jour* (1967), Catherine Deneuve is frigid around her respectful and affectionate husband, but when she imagines his having her tied to a tree and whipped, she is able to reach orgasm from feeling the force of his desire. Similarly, Kim Basinger in *9 1/2 Weeks* (1986) finally feels something that moves her in a world of soulless corporate greed and distantly hostile takeovers when Mickey Rourke makes her crawl across the floor on her hands and knees, picking up money while he cracks a whip. In *Lies* (*Kojitmal*, 1999), an older man (Lee Sang-Hyun) spanks, whips and tattoos a younger woman (Kim Tae-Yeon) in a desperate attempt to fix some indelible mark on her flesh to stand as proof of his desire once he predeceases her. And *In My Skin* (*Dans ma peau*, 2002) has the repressed Marina de Van forcing

Still from 'Love Is the Devil' (1998)
This stylized image of a man writhing in torment is from a film about painter Francis Bacon (Derek Jacobi) and his sadomasochistic art and life. "There's no beauty without the wound," says Bacon, and he wonders, "Is my lover to be my assassin, or I his?"

'The violence of death and sexual violence, when they are linked together, have this dual significance. On the one hand the convulsions of the flesh are more acute when they are near to a black-out, and on the other a black-out, as long as there is enough time, makes physical pleasure more exquisite.'

Georges Bataille, *Erotism: Death & Sensuality*

"You are here to serve your masters. Your hands are not your own, nor are your breasts, nor, most especially, any of your bodily orifices, which we may explore or penetrate at will."

Pauline Réage, ***The Story of O***

ABOVE
Still from 'Duel in the Sun' (1946)
The fiery love-hate relationship between Pearl Chavez (Jennifer Jones) and Lewt McCanles (Gregory Peck) ends when they shoot each other and then die together while expressing their love with their last breath.

OPPOSITE
Still from 'The Story of O' (1975)
Corinne Cléry consents to being shackled and then whipped. "Both this flogging and the chain... are intended less to make you suffer, scream, or shed tears than to make you feel, through this suffering, that you are not free but fettered." (Pauline Réage, 'The Story of O')

herself to open up a new world of pulsing sensation by penetrating her flesh with a knife and licking the gashes.

Sometimes masochism is about showing there is literally no limit to your love, about giving yourself over to the other – body and soul. In *The Story of O* (*Histoire d'O*, 1975), when Corinne Cléry obeys her lover and lets herself be taken both orally and anally, it is to prove that she has opened every orifice to her man, that he owns her entirely. When she allows herself to be tied up, whipped and branded with a hot iron, she is reducing herself to O, a mere receptacle for his burning pleasure, a nothing overwhelmed by his all. Similarly, Derek Jacobi in *Love is the Devil* (1998) feels that he exists entirely for the pleasure of another man when he allows his back to be burned with cigarettes and himself to be sodomized, or when he is strangled by his lover's hands during sex and choked by forced fellatio. What greater gift than to sacrifice the breath of life itself, to die from penetration? Leonardo Treviglio as *Sebastiane* (1976) ends up as a martyr to another man's desire when he is tied naked to a stake and pierced by arrows. As Anne McClintock notes, masochism is like Christianity in being about 'transcendence through mortification of the flesh: through self-abasement, the spirit finds release in an ecstasy of abandonment.'

Masochism can be a way of expressing ambivalence about the power of the other sex, a desire mixed with dread. In *Body of Evidence* (1993), lawyer Willem Dafoe is defending Madonna, a woman on trial for having screwed her lover to death. Fascinated yet fearful, Dafoe finds out just how much female heat he can take when she drips candle wax onto his chest. If a man feels too threatened by a woman's dominance, he may have sadistic fantasies of a power reversal. In *8 1/2* (1963), Marcello Mastroianni imagines taking a whip to his harem of mistresses when they rebel against having to serve him – a lashing he thinks some of them enjoy as much as he revels in giving it to them. Such mistreatment, though, may escalate the battle of the sexes, prompting women to inflict even more exquisite torture. When widower Ryo Ishibashi subjects Eihi Shiina to a fake *Audition* (*Odishon*, 1999) which is really a meat market for choosing a woman to bed, it is she who gives him the painful pleasure of being entered by a hypodermic needle and of having his flesh cut up by cheese wire.

For the warring couple whose excitement comes from ever-increasing levels of abuse, where will it end? In *Maîtresse* (1973), Gérard Depardieu's mistress, Bulle Ogier, is a dominatrix. The two of them fight each other for sexual supremacy by using the bodies of others as surrogate victims. Depardieu succeeds in spanking and belt-whipping a woman's bare bottom, but Ogier rather surpasses him by stubbing a cigarette into a man's hand, poking bamboo shoots into a man's ear, piercing a man's nipples with needles and nailing a man's penis to a board. The couple does reach a climactic balance of power in the end: both of them occupy the driver's seat of a speeding car, as she rides him and steers the wheel, while he takes her from behind and puts his foot to the gas pedal. Having achieved this perfect balance of dominant and submissive, controlling and out of control, they can die happy – the car crashes. Sadomasochism leads to another *Liebestod* in *Matador* (1986) when retired bullfighter Nacho Martínez, seeking the ultimate climax, consents to being stabbed in the neck by serial killer Assumpta Serna who, having thus achieved her greatest desire in life, promptly kills herself.

Sadomasochism is at least consensual. A more extreme form of erotic fantasy is rape, or being taken against one's will. Nancy Friday has written that 'Not one woman I have ever met actually wanted to be raped in reality; what she wanted

school shower room. For Patric, rape becomes a way of expressing closeted desires while also violently denying them. And for Jean-Hugues Anglade in *L'Homme blessé* (1983), who spends the entire film trailing and trying to find fulfilment with the man he longs for, his rape-murder of that man in the end is the climactic explosion of both angry frustration and pent-up desire.

Still from 'Salo, or The 120 Days of Sodom' (1976)
The libertine named Blangis (Paolo Bonacelli) contemplates the hymen whose sanctity he will invade.

Sado-Masochistic Relationships

Page 142 Top Left: '9 1/2 Weeks' (1986)
Kim Basinger is blindfolded by Mickey Rourke so that her other senses will be heightened to feel pleasure – and pain.

Page 142 Top Right: 'Seven Beauties' (1976)
Concentration camp inmate Giancarlo Giannini is forced to grovel at the feet of commander Shirley Stoler and to crawl between her legs to service her.

Page 142 Bottom: 'The Beast' (1974)
After a chase through the woods, aristocratic beauty Sirpa Lane finds that she likes being caught and devoured by the beast in this erotic version of the fairy tale.

Page 143 Top Left: 'Nowhere' (1997)
Chiara Mastroianni and Debi Mazar are fully equipped to help James Duval indulge his sadomasochistic fantasies.

Page 143 Top Right: 'Pola X' (1999)
Guillaume Depardieu seizes the moment when Delphine Chuillot is in the middle of taking off her shirt to kiss her 'bound' body and 'veiled' face in this scene with S&M undertones.

Page 143 Bottom: 'Swept Away' (1975)
Seaman Giancarlo Giannini brings haughty Mariangela Melato down to earth for a passionate clinch on the beach in this battle-of-the-sexes film.

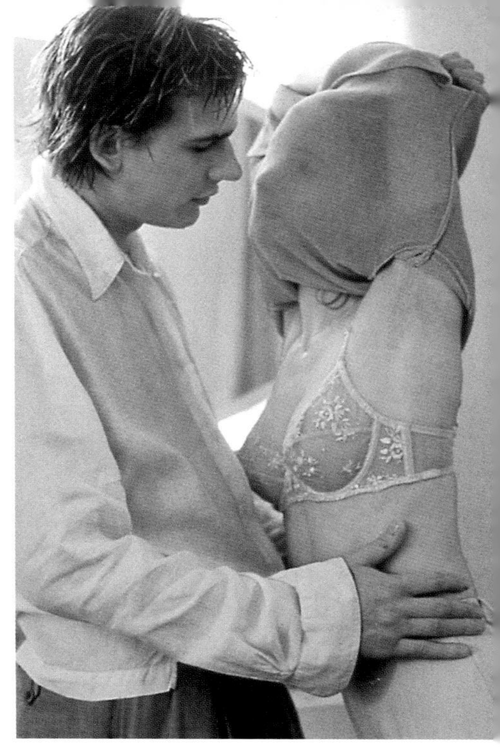

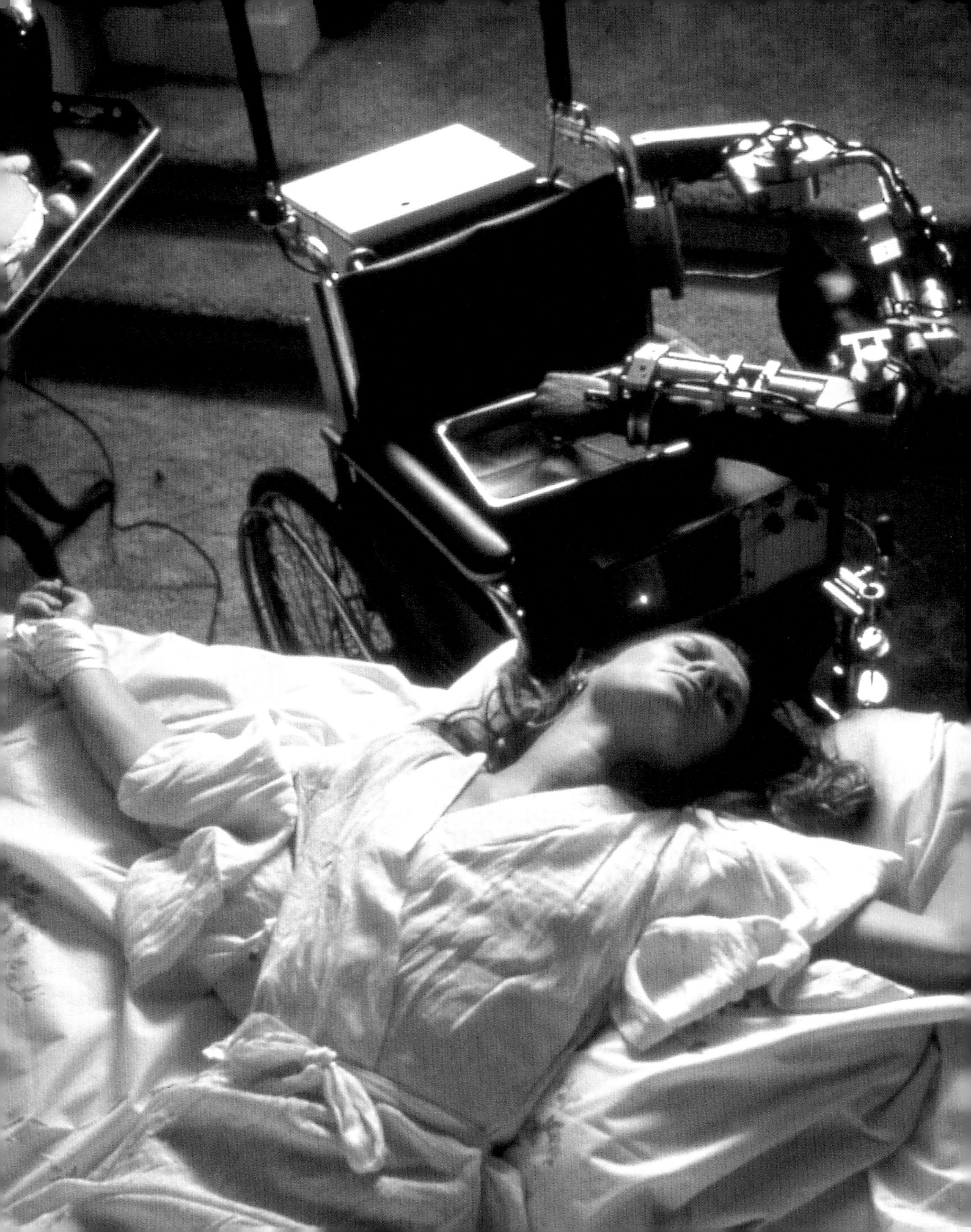

ABOVE

Still from 'Baise-moi' (2000)

In this rape-revenge film, Karen Bach and Raffaëla Anderson turn their phallic guns against the men who have wronged them, including shooting one in the anus.

LEFT

Still from 'The Damned' (1969)

Having felt emasculated by her for years, Helmut Berger finally rises up against his mother Ingrid Thulin and rapes her.

OPPOSITE

Still from 'Demon Seed' (1977)

Julie Christie is about to be raped by a computer that wants to impregnate her and seed a new kind of artificial intelligence.

ABOVE
Still from 'The Night Porter' (1974)
Concentration camp inmate Lucia (Charlotte Rampling) does a "Sieg Heil!" salute in long black gloves as she performs topless before a Nazi audience.

RIGHT
Still from 'The Night Porter' (1974)
SS officer Max (Dirk Bogarde) kisses the wounded arm of Lucia after he has had her injured.

One popular source for sadomasochistic eroticism on film has been Nazism. In *The Night Porter* (1974), Max (Dirk Bogarde) is a former SS officer who, 12 years after the end of the war, is keeping a low profile by working nights as a hotel porter in Vienna. When Lucia (Charlotte Rampling), a former concentration camp inmate, shows up at his hotel, the two of them begin to re-enact the master/slave relationship they had in the camp, with Lucia seeming to submit willingly to Max's domination. The film drew a firestorm of protest from feminists who resented the implication that women crave sexual humiliation and torture by men, and from Jewish groups who decried the idea that concentration camp victims secretly wanted to be abused by their Nazi captors.

Certainly, one understanding of Max and Lucia's actions is to see them as having been so traumatized by the past that they are now obsessively repeating it. In this view, the two simply take up their old positions again, reliving such scenes as when Max played the sadistic voyeur filming a stripped-naked Lucia, or when he had her dress like a child so that he could molest his "little girl". But things are not so simple. As director Liliana Cavani points out about one incident in Max and Lucia's past, "He had her arm subjected to torture so that he could kiss her wounds gently." There was a sensory intensity to the pains and pleasures they experienced in the wartime concentration camp that nothing in the dull, peaceful present can match, and so even Lucia consents to re-enact these moments of torture and tenderness. More than that, the two begin to reverse roles, with Lucia as the dominatrix and Max as one who willingly accepts punishment out of guilt over what he did to her in the past. Lucia smashes a perfume bottle and has Max press his bare foot onto the broken glass, much as he had earlier injured her arm. In the changing power dynamic of their sadomasochistic relationship, it is not clear who is really the slave and who the master. This erotic tension is epitomized in the scene where a bare-breasted Lucia vamps Max by performing a cabaret number in long black gloves and a Nazi cap. He is the SS officer, but she has made him her sexual slave.

"The colour is black, the material is leather, the seduction is beauty, the justification is honesty, the aim is ecstasy, the fantasy is death."

Susan Sontag, 'Fascinating Fascism'

Still from 'The Night Porter' (1974)
Max and Lucia re-enact their sadomasochistic relationship in the present. The movie's director and stars were tried on obscenity charges, though eventually acquitted when such respected film-makers as Luchino Visconti and Bernardo Bertolucci came to their defence.

Ménage à Trois / Orgy

Researcher Alfred C. Kinsey once defined a nymphomaniac as 'someone who has more sex than you do'. Kinsey shocked readers when he revealed in his 1953 study of *Sexual Behavior and the Human Female* that, among the 6,000 women he surveyed, 26% had had extramarital affairs, 50% had had premarital intercourse and 14% regularly had multiple orgasms. This was the 1950s and, unlike men, women were still considered to have low or no libidos – that is, if they were proper ladies and good mothers. While men had strong sex drives so that they could sow their wild oats, women were supposedly natural pair-bonders whose meagre desires were fully satisfied by one man. Science writer Catherine Blackledge tells us that 'until recently, the females of many species were said to be monogamous, preferring to mate with only one male. This theory has now been shown to be wrong – females of the majority of species are polygamous, choosing to mate with multiple males.'

Before the enforcement of the censorious Production Code in 1934, some female characters gave free rein to their carnal appetites. In *Baby Face* (1933), Barbara Stanwyck seduces one man after another as she sleeps her way to the top of a high-rise office building, while Ruth Chatterton in *Female* (1933) is a company president who uses her male employees to satisfy her urges in a series of one-night stands. Pre-Code women lay claim to the same desires as men – and the same right to wander if they find that men are unfaithful. When her husband cheats on her, Norma Shearer sleeps with his best friend and declares unrepentantly, "I'm glad I discovered there's more than one man in the world, while I'm young enough and they want me. I'm not missing anything from now on." (*The Divorcee*, 1930) And when Shearer is jilted by her lover in *Strangers May Kiss* (1931), she takes lovers of her own all over Europe, prompting one observer to say that "She changes her men with her lingerie, that girl."

Of course, women in these films were having way too much fun, and so the censors stepped in to curtail their sexual freedom. One such critic wrote that Shearer 'personifies the warped moral sense that has disintegrated every previous civilized nation'. Liberated lust had to be punished. In *The Road to Ruin* (1928), high-school girl Helen Foster finds that premarital sex leads to being abandoned by her lover, being prostituted to a man who turns out to be her father and being killed by a botched abortion. In *The Chapman Report* (1962), nymphomaniac Claire Bloom receives 'poetic justice' in a gang rape (the first in a Hollywood film).

Still from 'Scandal' (1989)
Joanne Whalley-Kilmer plays high-class prostitute Christine Keeler, whose liaison with a British defence minister and a Russian military attaché led to the minister's resignation.

"For me, love is very deep. Sex only has to go a few inches."

Stacy Nelkin, *Bullets Over Broadway* (1994)

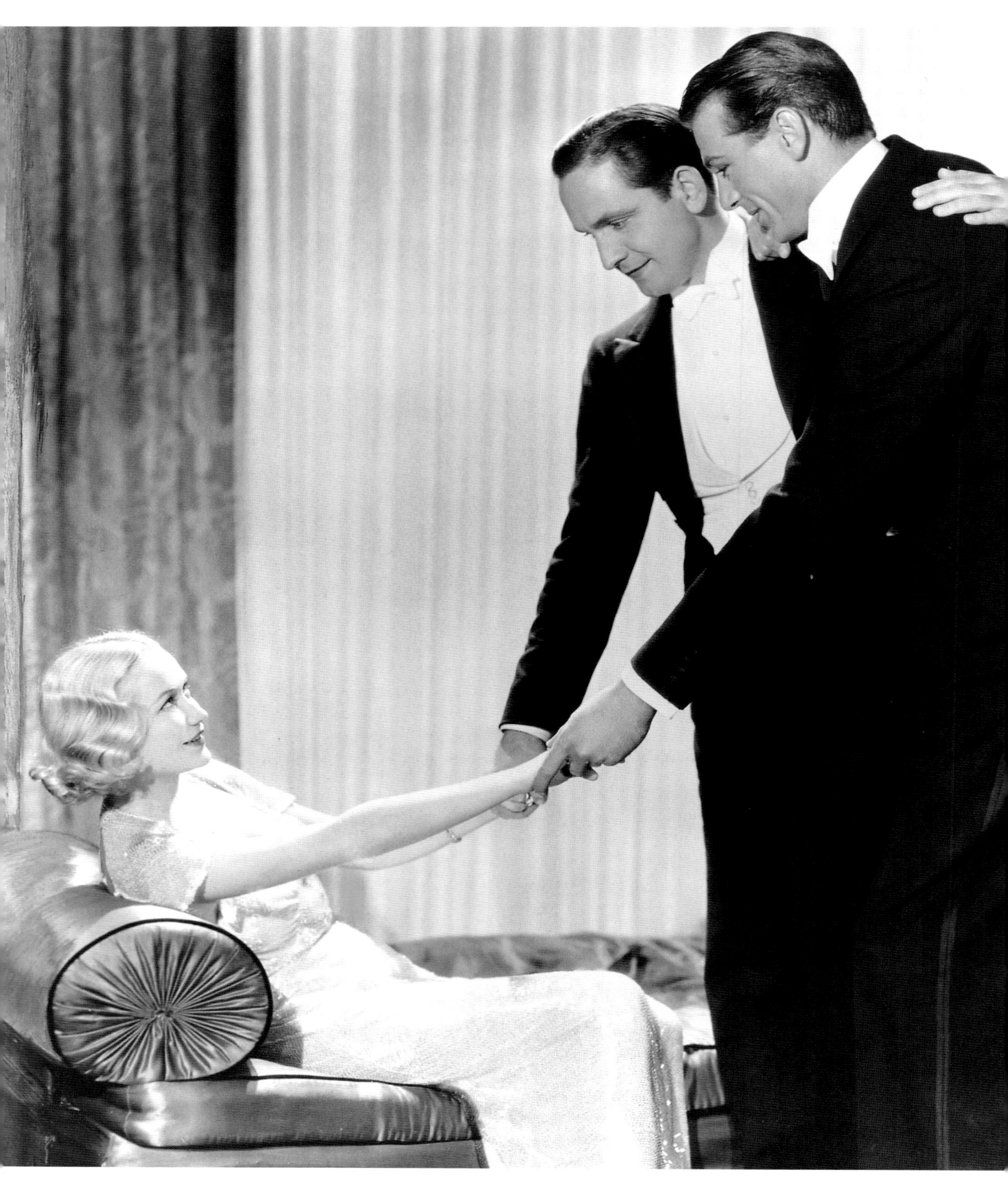

ABOVE

Still from 'Bob & Carol & Ted & Alice' (1969)

Elliot Gould & Natalie Wood & Robert Culp & Dyan Cannon are two married couples who try mate-swapping. Note that this scene follows the Sticky Sheet rule, as identified by David Stevens: 'The large seam at the top edge of sheets used in movies is covered with a sex-specific adhesive, causing the sheet to stick firmly to the upper breast area of women, while inches away, the same sheet clings above the man's waist.'

LEFT

Still from 'Rebel Without a Cause' (1955)

Alienated from adult society, teenage rebels Plato (Sal Mineo), Jim (James Dean) and Judy (Natalie Wood) form a close-knit bond. Actor Sal Mineo once said about James Dean, "We never became lovers, but we could have – like that."

OPPOSITE

Still from 'Design for Living' (1933)

Why should free-spirited Miriam Hopkins choose between playwright Fredric March and painter Gary Cooper when she can have them both?

ABOVE
Still from 'The Dreamers' (2003)
Matthew (Michael Pitt) begins sleeping with Isabelle (Eva Green), who has often curled up naked in bed with her brother Theo (Louis Garrel). In the original novel on which this film was based, Matthew gets together with Theo, too.

RIGHT
Still from 'A Zed & Two Noughts' (1985)
Double amputee Andréa Ferréol has her two 'legs' provided by twins Brian and Eric Deacon. She sleeps with both of them and becomes pregnant – with twins!

But the tide would turn again, and the feminist revolution of the late 1960s and 1970s would encourage women to insist on their right to sexual self-determination. In *Barbarella* (1968), Jane Fonda's limitless capacity for multiple orgasms burns up the Excess Pleasure Machine that a male villain tries to use to torture her. In *She's Gotta Have It* (1986), Nora Darling takes her pleasure with three male lovers and resists their attempts to pin her down to one. And in *Warm Water Under a Red Bridge* (*Akai Hashi No Shita No Nurui Mizu*, 2001), Misa Shimizu exhibits her female sexual power by gushing a great flood when she climaxes, overwhelming her male partner with wonder and some fear.

While sexually adventurous women have sometimes been stigmatized as 'whores' or 'nymphomaniacs', lustful males have had an easier time with the censor, perhaps because men are expected to be randy and to play the field. Consider the envy that many felt for Errol Flynn, the swashbuckling star whom David Niven once described as "a magnificent specimen of the rampant male". Flynn's swordsmanship both on-screen and off was much admired, and his success with so many ladies led to the popular catch-phrase, "in like Flynn". But concerns about male promiscuity can be seen in *Alfie* (1966), which finds lusty humour in Michael Caine's portrayal of a Cockney Casanova yet also pathos in the women he loves and leaves behind. By the time we get to *Fellini's Casanova* (1976), Donald Sutherland as the legendary lover has become an exhausted sex machine, his buttocks pumping mechanically on top of woman after woman in a desperate attempt to prove his virility.

For others, though, the appeal of sleeping around is in the novelty and variety of partners. But what if you could enjoy your additional bedmates simultaneously rather than serially? Some film characters find that a ménage à trois compounds their pleasure. There is an implied threesome involving adulterous desire in *Blow-Up* (1966) when, as her husband is on top of her making love, Sarah Miles sees another man (David Hemmings) at a window and silently begs him to stay so that she can

"Your idea of fidelity is not having more than one man in bed at the same time."

Dirk Bogarde to Julie Christie, *Darling* (1965)

Still from 'Savage Nights' (1992)
Bisexual director Cyril Collard (on the right) has sex with both aspiring actress Romane Bohringer and skinhead soccer player Carlos López.

reach orgasm while looking at his face. A suggested threesome has homoerotic overtones in *Bully* (2001) where Nick Stahl's idea of foreplay in bed with his girlfriend is to have them watch a video of his buddy Brad Renfro, and where Stahl later pulls Renfro off another girl and takes his place inside her. In *1900* (1977), Robert De Niro and Gérard Depardieu are young men lying on either side of a prostitute in bed while she gives them simultaneous hand jobs, and De Niro reaches over to give his friend's member a helping hand.

From the woman's perspective, a ménage à trois can offer freedom from the constraints of marriage and the limitations of having to settle for only one kind of man. At the end of *Design for Living* (1933), Miriam Hopkins leaves her possessive husband and takes a seat in a cab between intellectual Fredric March and manly Gary Cooper, kissing each of her two lovers and getting the best of both worlds. Free-spirited Jeanne Moreau refuses to choose between *Jules and Jim* (*Jules et Jim*, 1962), marrying Oskar Werner while remaining the mistress of Henri Serre. She gives her love to both of them while retaining her independence like one of the guys, as in the scene where, dressed in baggy pants with suspenders and a moustache, she runs across a bridge flanked by her two men. And in *Doña Flor and Her Two Husbands* (*Doña Flor e Seus Dois Maridos*, 1976), Sonia Braga is glad when the ghost of her dead first husband (José Wilker) materializes to make passionate love to her, while she also gets to keep her second, living husband (Mauro Mendoça) who may be boring but who, unlike the first, is faithful and a good provider.

More recent films depict the ménage à trois as even more explicitly transgressive and liberating. At the end of *Ken Park* (2002), Tiffany Limos tries to create a sensual paradise of total fulfilment by positioning herself between Stephen Jasso and James Bullard, taking one of them orally and the other vaginally. In the opening scene of *Black and White* (1999), Bijou Phillips, Kim Matulova and Oliver "Power" Grant – two girls and a guy – are intertwined while standing up, their clothes in disarray, making love together in a public park. Although the MPAA ratings board claimed to object to Phillips' arm movements which suggest she is masturbating Grant, director James Toback believes that "What really bothered them is that it's a scene of interracial and intragender sex."

If a threesome is transgressive, then an orgy is revolutionary – or at least that's the idea in *The Idiots* (*Idioterne*, 1998) where a guerrilla group misbehaves in public places, protesting bourgeois conventions by baring female breasts, exhibiting erections and finally having group sex – with real penetrations which prompted US censors to place black bars over the orgiastic organs so that bourgeois viewers would not be offended. *Zabriskie Point* (1970) climaxes with a group 'love-in' as sex between the film's main couple expands into a mind-blowing shot of hundreds of couples and threesomes making out among the sand dunes.

In other films, unbridled carnal appetite leads to satiety and suicide. At Trimalchio's banquet in *Fellini's Satyricon* (1969), guests cram their mouths with food while feasting their eyes on female flesh, and in *La grande bouffe* (1973) four men spend an entire weekend whoring and gorging themselves to death. But orgiastic excess really runs riot when Malcolm McDowell as *Caligula* (1978) incites his subjects to pursue their lust for power and pleasure. One woman sits on a phallic swing; another lowers a snake toward her vagina; a third is penetrated by a man in a horned mask; and a fourth rides the erection of a man who has just been killed. McDowell asserts *droit du seigneur*, raping a bride in front of her groom and then taking the groom's anal virginity with a finger. McDowell also fondles and brings a

"Sex is nobody's business except the three people involved."

Tallulah Bankhead

OPPOSITE TOP LEFT
Still from 'Performance' (1970)
"You never feel female? That's what's wrong with you, isn't it?" Anita Pallenberg dresses up macho gangster James Fox in a woman's clothes and wig to help him get in touch with his feminine side.

OPPOSITE TOP RIGHT
Still from 'Performance' (1970)
The genders seem to bend and intertwine in this lovemaking scene where Anita Pallenberg (in the centre) shares a bed with long-haired Mick Jagger (left) and boyish-breasted Michèle Breton (right).

OPPOSITE BOTTOM
Still from 'Performance' (1970)
Is the character standing at the right a male or a female? It is in fact actress Michèle Breton, but androgyny is the point of this bathtub scene where Mick Jagger, Anita Pallenberg and Michèle Breton find that genders blend in the sensual flow.

ABOVE
Still from 'Casanova' (1927)
"If all those sweet young things present were laid end to end, I wouldn't be at all surprised," as Dorothy Parker once said about Hollywood starlets and the casting couch. In this scene, legendary lover Casanova (Ivan Mosjoukine) has bedded all these nude beauties.

OPPOSITE TOP
Still from 'Fellini's Satyricon' (1969)
Flesh of all kinds is on the menu at Trimalchio's banquet in this orgiastic scene of dining and debauchery.

OPPOSITE BOTTOM
Still from 'Caligula' (1978)
Caligula (Malcolm McDowell) is taken on a tour of a Roman orgy by Tiberius (Peter O'Toole). "They lust for power and pleasure," says Tiberius, and the movie certainly gives us an eyeful of both.

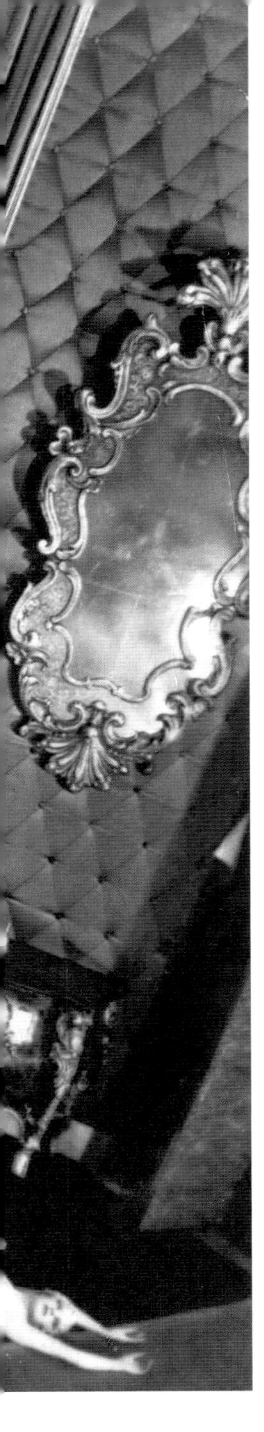

ABOVE
Still from 'The Story of O' (1975)
Young women dine freely in a civilized setting, but their bondage is indicated by the leather collars they wear. Each collar has a key that any man can use whenever he desires to gain entrance to a woman.

RIGHT
Still from 'Behind the Green Door' (1972)
Marilyn Chambers is "loved as never before" in this scene where multiple partners attend to her every orifice and erogenous zone.

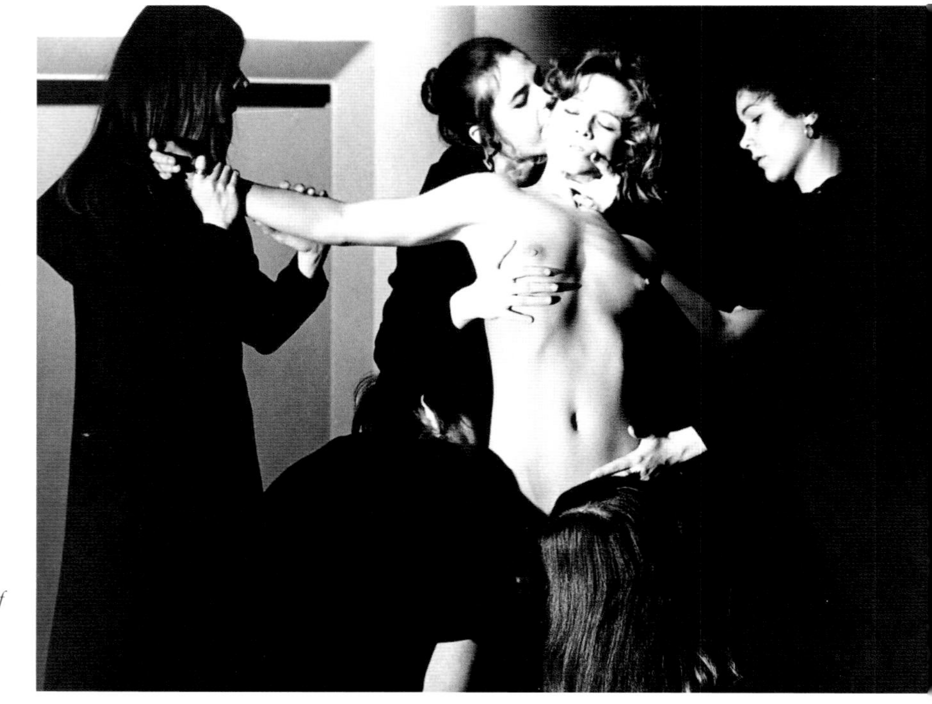

"Sexuality is limited by taboos, and the domain of eroticism is that of the transgression of these taboos."

Georges Bataille

ABOVE

Still from 'Zabriskie Point' (1970)

The orgy in the sand dunes at the end of this swinging 1960s film signals the advent of a new era of free love. This was a little too much freedom for the ratings board, which almost slapped the film with an X rating.

LEFT

Still from 'Behind the Green Door' (1972)

Love is contagious: the audience members at a sex show can't help breaking out into an orgy of their own, which presumably cues us to do likewise.

'If you are shocked or embarrassed by total nudity and sexual activity, you are urged not to attend!'

From the ad for *The Depraved* (*Exponerad*, 1971)

ABOVE
Still from 'Y tu mamá también' (2001)
Luisa (Maribel Verdú) has to tell the inexperienced Tenoch (Diego Luna) to take her panties off before he goes down on her.

RIGHT
Still from 'Y tu mamá también' (2001)
Overeager Julio (Gael García Bernal) reaches climax too quickly when he has sex in the backseat of a car with Luisa.

'Like a boy who hesitates to explore a haunted house alone, these men feel more excited, sexually more courageous – more like men – *if when they are having sex with a woman, another man is there, too.'*

Nancy Friday, *Men in Love: Men's Sexual Fantasies*

horse to bed, caresses his sister's dead body and gets pleasure from watching wooden stakes being driven into a woman's nether region. It takes a special sort of person to find these scenes in *Caligula* erotic.

Most hardcore porn films try to present orgies in a more positive light, using them to show that women's desires are as strong as men's, that sex with anyone and everyone is good and that one can never get enough of a good thing. Porn turns the censor's scorn to erotic ends, making guilt fuel the flames of lust, and what sex is more sinful than the insatiable kind that leads to an orgy? In *The Devil in Miss Jones* (1972), repressed spinster Georgina Spelvin finds herself in Hell after committing suicide, but since she is there anyway, she asks for some additional time on earth so that she can enjoy committing enough sexual sins to deserve damnation – sins which include an orgy in which she is fulfilled both vaginally and anally at the same time. And Marilyn Chambers – formerly the Ivory Snow detergent box girl – finds no end of dirty delights *Behind the Green Door* (1973). When she has sex on stage with four guys at once – one in each hand, one in her mouth, and one in her vagina – the male and female voyeurs in the audience grow so excited that they too start copulating and the entire room comes together in one big orgy.

One of the most popular non-pornographic explorations of a threesome in recent years is *Y tu mamá también* (2001), directed by Alfonso Cuarón. In this film, Tenoch (Diego Luna) and Julio (Gael García Bernal) are two horny Mexican teens accompanied on their beach vacation by a gorgeous Spanish woman, Luisa (Maribel Verdú). They just want to score with her and each boy does in separate scenes, but she helps them to grow toward emotional – and not just sexual – maturity, encouraging the diffident Tenoch to let her see his naked member, and prompting the overeager Julio to take it easy and to look at her face during sex. Unfortunately, the macho boys begin to fight in jealous rivalry, each laying sole claim to Luisa and each bragging about having slept with the other's girlfriend back home in Mexico City. Julio even claims to have been with Tenoch's mother – the ultimate insult which gives the film its title, "And your mother, too!" In the end, though, Luisa

brings the boys together in a scene where she dances sandwiched between them at a cantina. Later, in her hotel room, she has them stand side by side, undoes their trousers, and fellates them both, while they turn to kissing and embracing each other.

Still from 'Y tu mamá también' (2001)
Julio, Luisa and Tenoch do a sensual dance together before taking their threesome into the bedroom.

'[In a male-female-male threesome] the presence of the woman enables the man to express his homoerotic needs while being able to avoid facing them at the same time.'

Nancy Friday, *Men in Love: Men's Sexual Fantasies*

Sexual Intercourse

In *Take the Money and Run* (1969), Woody Allen says, "The psychiatrist asked me if I thought sex was dirty and I said, 'It is if you're doing it right.'" Having sex for pleasure – and not just for procreation – always seems forbidden, as if it breaks some kind of parental, societal or religious rule. Most films don't show sex directly: shots of penetration and intercourse will get a movie effectively banned from most theatres; sex is X-rated. But precisely because sex cannot be shown, everything around it is eroticized. Anything approaching sex takes on the frisson of the forbidden. One way that movies capitalize on this erotic tension is through suggestive dialogue. "I'm just a nice young woman – not too young and not too nice, I hope" is Greta Garbo's flirtatious line in *Inspiration* (1931). Ginger Rogers is slightly more forward about what she wants, while remaining safely within the realm of the symbolic, when she says to a *Young Man of Manhattan* (1930), "Cigarette me, big boy." Elizabeth Ashley positions us to use our imaginations when she answers a question about what she would like to see on her honeymoon by saying, "Lots and lots of lovely ceilings" (*The Carpetbaggers*, 1964). And Mae West's line – "Thanks, I enjoyed every inch of it" – is all the more salacious for not specifying what "it" is.

Along with verbal indirection, films also use visual symbolism to approach – while not actually showing – sex. This works especially well in scenes of sexual frustration, where the characters approach fulfilment of their desires but hit an obstacle. In *Splendor in the Grass* (1961), teenagers Warren Beatty and Natalie Wood are parked in lovers' lane, engaged in passionate kissing and heavy breathing. She suddenly grows fearful of sex, pleading for him to stop, but the gushing waterfall behind them continues as evidence of their desire for climax. In *From Here to Eternity* (1953), Burt Lancaster and Deborah Kerr are wearing bathing suits while engaged in an upper-body embrace on the beach, but the spume from the crashing waves rolling over them suggests a more complete fulfilment. Another scene where sex is not shown but the whole environment is eroticized occurs in *Body Heat* (1981) which has William Hurt, on a sizzling hot night, standing outside glass doors looking lustfully in at Kathleen Turner and then breaking in with a chair, while she moans, "Do it!" Photographer David Hemmings and supermodel Veruschka might as well be doing it in *Blow-Up* (1966) when he points his long lens at her, straddles her and then takes photos of her writhing on the floor. Just as Cary Grant and Eva Marie Saint begin to make love in *North by Northwest* (1959), the train they are on

Still from 'Sex & Lucía' (2001)
For some viewers, this shot of bouncy free spirit Paz Vega straddling a motorbike is more erotic than any explicit sex scene.

"There may be some things better than sex, and some things may be worse, but there is nothing exactly like it."

W.C. Fields

ABOVE

Still from 'I Am Curious (Yellow)' (1967)

Lena Nyman makes love with Börje Ahlstedt as part of her in-depth survey of sexual attitudes and activities in Sweden. He is the 24th man she has slept with, but she says that "the first 19 were no fun."

RIGHT

Still from 'I Am Curious (Yellow)' (1967)

This film's relatively explicit sex scenes – including an erection and cunnilingus – challenged obscenity laws and expanded the boundaries of what it was permissible to show on screen, leading eventually to hardcore films that would show penetration and ejaculation.

ABOVE

Still from 'I Am Curious (Yellow)' (1967)

The film's sex scenes were shot in black-and-white documentary style. Some found their gritty realism to be frankly erotic, while for others such as critic William Rotsler, the sex scenes were 'deadly dull and about as erotic as a flooded gopher hole.'

LEFT

On the Set of 'I Am Curious (Yellow)' (1967)

Director Vilgot Sjöman gives instruction to his actors Lena Nyman and Börje Ahlstedt, telling them to "break away from the ordinary way of presenting very arranged love scenes, and to approach reality".

ABOVE
Still from 'Mandingo' (1975)
When a white plantation owner takes a slave woman as his mistress, his neglected wife (Susan George) gets revenge and satisfies her lust with a male slave (Ken Norton).

RIGHT
Still from 'Mandingo' (1975)
A woman checks out the studly merchandise at a slave market, and Ken Norton has little choice but to smile.

heads into a tunnel, while in *Beyond the Valley of the Dolls* (1970) a man lies on top of a woman and there is a cut-away at mid-thrust to a pumping oil derrick.

If visually and verbally suggesting sex has a certain taboo-breaking thrill, then how much more exciting is it when that sex is adulterous? The censors' 1930 Production Code expressly barred films from presenting adultery 'as attractive or alluring' – a prohibition which only served to set a transgressive cinematic agenda for years to come. 'The sanctity of the institution of marriage and the home shall be upheld,' says the Production Code, while John Malkovich in *Dangerous Liaisons* (1988) plots to seduce a married woman: "I want her to believe in God and virtue and the sanctity of marriage, and still not be able to stop herself. I want the excitement of watching her betray everything that's most important to her." In *The Girl Can't Help It* (1956), when newlywed Jayne Mansfield shows affection to another man, Tom Ewell tells her, "That's no way for a bride to act." "I thought brides acted that way," she says, to which he replies, "Only with the groom." *Indecent Proposal* (1993) is all about breaking the sanctity of marriage. After Robert Redford offers to pay her one million dollars to sleep with him, Demi Moore and her husband Woody Harrelson make love on a bed covered with bills, turned on by her whorish transgression.

Indeed, part of the thrill of adultery lies in flouting the rule of monogamy. "I finally discovered the difference between a husband and a lover – night and day," says one savvy woman in *Critic's Choice* (1963). Of course, what is good for the goose is good for the gander. Asked whether he talks to his wife during sex, one man says, "Yes, if I happen to be near the phone." (*If You Don't Stop It...You'll Go Blind*, 1978) A man on the phone with his wife while having sex with his mistress is

White Madeline Kahn: "Is it true what they say about how you people are built? Oh, it's true, it's true!"
Black Cleavon Little: "Excuse me, ma'am, I hate to disillusion you, but you're sucking on my arm."

Blazing Saddles (1974)

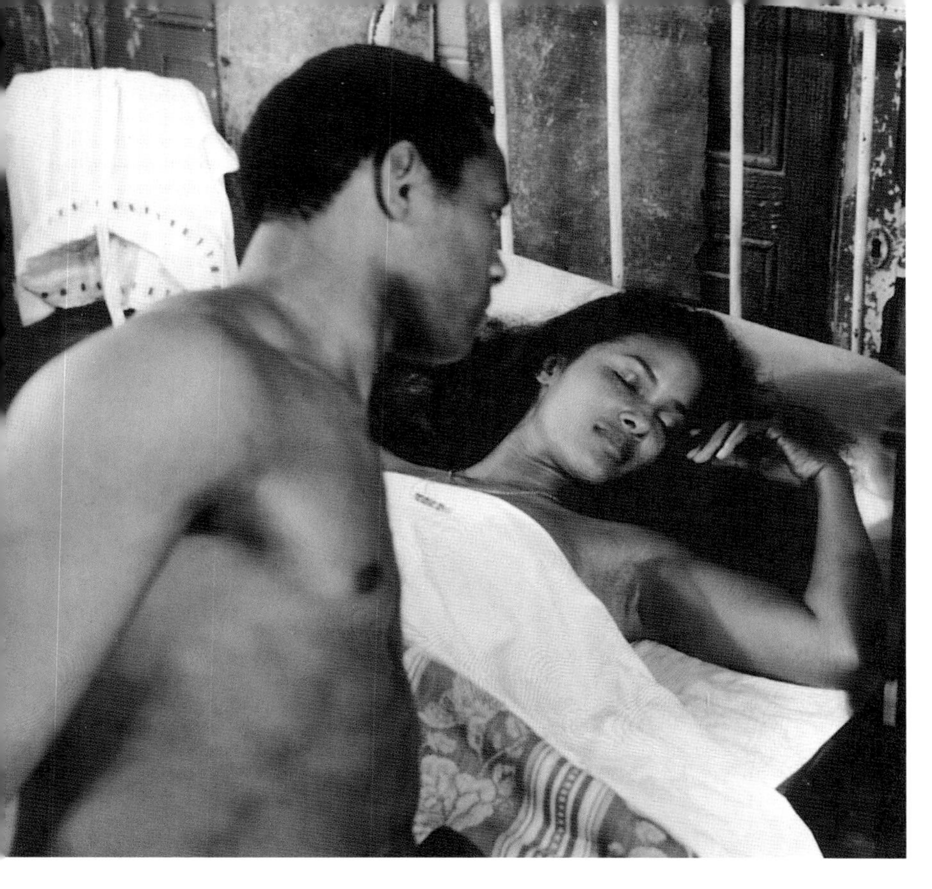

engaged in a kind of secret threesome. Sometimes the phantom presence of a lover can spice up marital sex. In *The Key* (*La chiave*, 1973), Frank Finlay is inflamed by jealousy over his wife Stefania Sandrelli's affair with a lover, pawing each part of her body and demanding, "Did he touch you here?" And when Balthazar Getty has pounding sex with faithful girlfriend Natasha Gregson Wagner in the backseat of a car in *Lost Highway* (1997), his thrusts are driven by thoughts of another woman, Patricia Arquette, the true object of his lust.

Infidelity also entails the fear of discovery, which can be a powerful aphrodisiac. Bold in his white T-shirt, Paul Newman in *Hud* (1963) walks up behind housekeeper Patricia Neal and snakes his arms around her. When she reprimands him for not asking first, he says, "Honey, the only question I ever ask any woman is, 'What time is your husband coming home?'" In *The Decameron* (1971), a husband does come home at an inconvenient time for his wife and her lover, but she quickly hides the man and then convinces her spouse to work on scraping out a large jar while her lover gets busy again with her own jar. In *The Canterbury Tales* (*I racconti di Canterbury*, 1972), a poor farmer in need of a mare is foolish enough to let his wife be turned into one by another man who gives her his "tail", while elsewhere a blind old man unwittingly aids in his own cuckolding when his wife has him bend over so that she can use his back to climb up to her lover in a tree. Adultery is less ribald and more dire in *Proof of Life* (2000), in which Russell Crowe plays a ransom expert hired to help Meg Ryan get her kidnapped husband back. In a segment cut from the film, Crowe and Ryan have adulterous sex and just as she screams out in climax, we see her husband's leg being pierced by a bamboo spear as he is trying to escape from his captors. The lovers' illicit joy blends with the husband's pain.

ABOVE

Poster for 'How to Make Love to a Negro Without Getting Tired' (1989)

Black penis size is seen through the magnifying mirror – or refracted through the myth – of white fears and desires in this satirical Canadian film.

LEFT

Still from 'Black Orpheus' (1959)

Breno Mello and Marpessa Dawn re-enact the tragic love story of Orpheus and Eurydice against a sensuous Brazilian backdrop of warm tropical light, colourful carnival costumes, and a blue-green sea.

'I fail to see any special merit in penises of more than the usual size…In this, as in everything else, quality is more to be considered than quantity. It is the searching, not the splitting weapon that is of use.'

Mark Twain

RIGHT
Still from 'Don't Look Now' (1973)
Julie Christie and Donald Sutherland dress for dinner after making love. By cutting back and forth between the sex (before) and the dressing (after), the film imbues their lovemaking with the passion and poignancy of impending separation and sadness.

BELOW
Still from 'Don't Look Now' (1973)
For its time, this was an unusually explicit love scene to feature two mainstream stars (Donald Sutherland and Julie Christie), giving rise to much speculation about whether the actors were having sex for real.

LEFT

Still from 'Don't Look Now' (1973)

After sex with her husband, Julie Christie stands apart, thinking about death (the recent drowning of their daughter) and the possibility of new life. Director Nicolas Roeg has said that he "wanted the feeling that at that moment of making love she might have become pregnant again."

BELOW

Still from 'Don't Look Now' (1973)

Perhaps the most shocking thing about this sex scene is that it depicts passionate love between a middle-aged married couple. Such steamy scenes usually occur only between horny teenage virgins or older adulterous lovers.

"It was incredibly bizarre, because I met the actress, Toni Kalem, right before the love scene. And she pulled me into her trailer... and we were both very giggly about it and like, 'Hi, how are you? I'll be fucking you in about five minutes in front of 50 people, and what's your name?'"

Aidan Quinn talking about acting in *Reckless* (1984)

Still from 'Body Heat' (1981)
William Hurt and Kathleen Turner try to cool their passion in a bathtub full of ice water. She: "My temperature runs a couple of degrees high, around a hundred. It's the engine or something." He: "Maybe you need a tune-up." She: "Don't tell me – you have just the right tool."

Adultery was not the only threat to traditional marriage singled out by the censors. The Production Code also warned film-makers that 'Miscegenation (sex relationships between the white and black races) is forbidden.' In the white imagination, black men were often seen as embodying a primitive potency that both threatens and thrills civilization. In *The Birth of a Nation* (1915), as much shivery pleasure as possible is wrung out of the scene where a bestial black chases and rapes a virginal white woman, and *King Kong* (1933) has the big black ape peel the dress off a writhing Fay Wray, probe her with his giant finger, and then sniff it. In *Live and Let Die* (1973), a black voodoo dancer holds a snake in his hand and extends it toward the mouth of virginal Jane Seymour. 'One is no longer aware of the Negro, but only of a penis: the Negro is eclipsed. He is turned into a penis. He *is* the penis,' writes psychoanalyst Frantz Fanon in describing such racist fantasies of fear and desire. And actress/model Tyra Banks has a similar complaint about filmic depictions of her sex: "Black women have always been these vixens, these animalistic erotic women. Why can't we just be the sexy American girl next door?" In *Angel Heart* (1987), black Lisa Bonet performs a voodoo dance in which she slits the throat of a chicken and has its blood spurt all over her body while she writhes orgasmically. Later, when white Mickey Rourke has intercourse with her in a hotel room to the tune of 'Soul on Fire', blood begins to rain down upon him. It is as if commingling with her dark race has brought on damnation.

Even pornographic films draw on racist myths to give sex a sense of transgressive excitement. In *Behind the Green Door* (1973), Marilyn Chambers is ravaged by black stud Johnny Keyes while he is wearing a bone necklace and war paint. Black actor/director Melvin Van Peebles both parodies and lays proud claim to these myths of black sexual prowess when he enters a screwing contest against a white biker gang and proves himself their superior at pleasuring a white woman in *Sweet Sweetback's Baadasssss Song* (1971). And *Mandingo* (1975), although much reviled for its racism, at least attempts to challenge some of these myths. It has a white plantation owner who sexually exploits his black slave mistress but then develops a tenderness toward her, and a neglected white wife who desires a black buck for his body and then begins to have feelings for him as a man.

The first film to challenge the censors' ban on interracial relationships was *Island in the Sun* (1957), and it did so in a timid way and according to a sexual double standard: white James Mason and black Dorothy Dandridge got to kiss, whereas black Harry Belafonte and white Joan Fontaine were restricted to holding hands, due to the greater fear of black male sexuality. Even in the year 1999, when director Mike Figgis wanted a black actor to play Adam and a white actress for Eve in his film *The Loss of Sexual Innocence*, the producers told him that "everything was fantastic" except for "one tiny detail... it's just about Adam. It's much better if he's white. Eve can be black." Reportedly, Whitney Houston and Kevin Costner filmed a steamy sex scene for *The Bodyguard* (1992), but it was cut due to fears that racial mixing would mean bad box office. Some say that Ellen Barkin and Laurence Fishburne made history in *Bad Company* (1994) by being the first interracial couple in a Hollywood film who have sex without mentioning race as an issue, but others believe that race – not sexual explicitness – was the reason that cuts were made in the scene where Barkin writhes ecstatically while straddling Fishburne on a chair. Perhaps *Monster's Ball* (2001) is the true landmark for the extraordinary realism and complexity of its interracial sex scene. Prison guard Billy Bob Thornton, who has had a racist upbringing, moves to take Halle Berry from behind as he is used to

ABOVE

Still from 'The Postman Always Rings Twice' (1981)

Adulterous lovers Frank (Jack Nicholson) and Cora (Jessica Lange) are so hot for each other that they have sex right on the kitchen table, amid the food and flour. Nicholson said that his co-star Lange was "like a delicate fawn, but crossed with a Buick".

LEFT

Still from 'The Postman Always Rings Twice' (1981)

Frank strips Cora for a roll in the hay. 'Cora seems to have a terrific orgasm as soon as Frank's dirty hand starts crawling up her thigh,' wrote Pauline Kael.

PAGES 172/173

Still from 'Against All Odds' (1984)

Making love in a variety of exotic South American locales, Jeff Bridges and Rachel Ward show a lot of skin in this steamy neo-noir remake of 'Out of the Past' (1947).

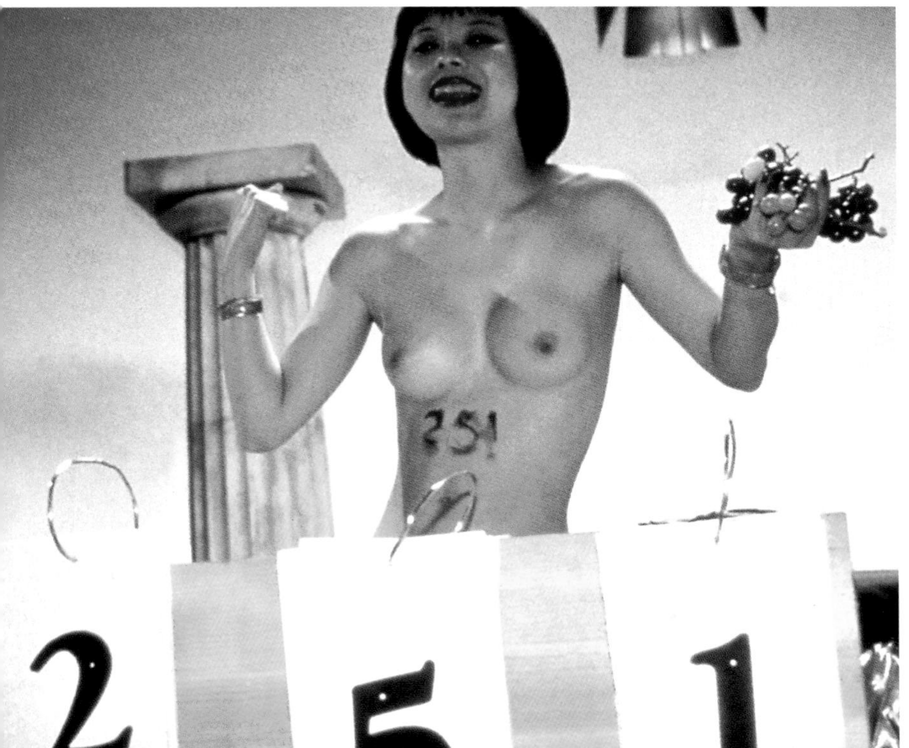

ABOVE
Still from 'Unfaithful' (2002)
Hunky French rare-book dealer Olivier Martinez must be something special indeed for Diane Lane to have an affair with him, considering that her husband is played by Richard Gere!

LEFT
Still from 'Sex: The Annabel Chong Story' (1999)
Gender studies student and porn star Annabel Chong has sex with 251 men in 10 hours.

OPPOSITE TOP
Still from 'Damage' (1992)
Adulterous lovers Juliette Binoche and Jeremy Irons oblivious to the pain they cause others. In real life, though, actor Jeremy Irons says that his wife "doesn't get jealous. When she sees me in sex scenes she says to herself, 'Oh, he is only acting. I know he can't last that long.'"

OPPOSITE BOTTOM
Still from 'Indecent Proposal' (1993)
Demi Moore and her husband are sexually excited by another man's proposal that she commit adultery for one million dollars.

"One of the pleasures of kinkier mainstream movies is that they jump-start our imaginations in a way that the familiar sweat-damp sexual wrestling of beautiful people has long since ceased to do."

Rebecca Traister

RIGHT
Still from 'Jamón, jamón' (1992)
Penélope Cruz rides a bucking Javier Bardem under the giant billboard of a bull in this film that both celebrates and satirizes macho potency.

BELOW
Still from 'Emmanuelle 2' (1975)
Emmanuelle (Sylvia Kristel) has sexual encounters with many men, but one of the most erotic is with her husband (Umberto Orsini), whom she still holds dear.

LEFT

Still from 'The Key' (1983)

In a comic scene that includes the sound of a whinnying horse, studly Franco Branciaroli is primed to mount Stefania Sandrelli, his future mother-in-law, in an affair sanctioned by her husband to fire up his own flagging libido.

BELOW

Still from 'The Decameron' (1971)

Caterina tells her parents that she is sleeping on the terrace to hear the song of the nightingale; actually, it is there that she meets her lover Riccardio. The next morning, her parents discover her with "the nightingale in her hand".

doing with prostitutes, but she leads him to adopt positions that will give her pleasure ("Make...me...feel...good"), including cunnilingus and woman on top. The scene is both thematically significant – he overcomes his racism – and realistically raw in its passion.

Racial differences are not the only ones that can add erotic friction to a scene. It is rubbing up against class boundaries that provides sexual tension in *Dirty Dancing* (1987), where working-class hunk Patrick Swayze and rich daddy's girl Jennifer Gray do the bump and grind to R&B music, dancing pelvis to pelvis with their hands, lips and legs all over each other. In *An Officer and a Gentleman* (1982), the class polarities are reversed but the sexual charge is the same. Factory worker Debra Winger is saved by naval officer Richard Gere in more ways than one, as in the scene where she slides on top of him in a chair, eases his manhood inside her, and rides him to freedom. And Leonardo DiCaprio plays a kid from steerage class who meets aristocratic lady Kate Winslet on the *Titanic* (1997). When the two find a car on board the ship, DiCaprio at first pretends to be Winslet's chauffeur ("Where to, Miss?"), but she whispers in his ear ("To the stars") and drags him into the backseat with her for some hot and heavy cross-class coupling. We see the ship's prow cleave through the water, the car windows steam up and Winslet's hand slam against the glass and then slide languorously down.

If breaching the class and colour divides can achieve a potent climax, then what would come from crossing the ultimate barrier – that between life and death? In *Against All Odds* (1984), Rachel Ward and Jeff Bridges find that deadly surroundings bring out their passion for life when they make love in a tomb of Aztec ruins. Danger fires up Eminem and Brittany Murphy when they have unprotected sex among heavy machinery in *8 Mile* (2002), and Ralph Fiennes and Julianne Moore choose to make fervent love while wartime bombs are falling rather than go to a shelter, even though doing so may mean *The End of the Affair* (1999). Some loves are so strong they push up against the end itself, refusing to die before climax. In *Leaving Las Vegas* (1995), suicidal alcoholic Nicolas Cage is on his deathbed, but Elisabeth Shue helps him to achieve an erection, mounts him, and moves him to orgasm just before he expires. In *Quills* (2000), Kate Winslet has died before Joaquin Phoenix is able to express his love for her, but he pulls the winding sheet from her naked body and climbs on top of her, imagining that she wraps her legs around him and returns his kisses – even though he is actually engaged in necrophilia. And *Kissed* (1996) has funeral-home attendant Molly Parker so attracted to a handsome male accident victim on the embalming table that she removes her clothes, climbs up and eases herself onto his body. When Parker's neglected boyfriend Peter Outerbridge discovers her love of death, he hangs himself to be with her in the way that she desires.

But director Nagisa Oshima's *In the Realm of the Senses* (*Ai No Corrida*, 1976) presents perhaps the deepest exploration of a love unto death. In the first half of the film, an inn owner named Kichi (Tatsuya Fuji) and his maid-turned-lover Sada (Eiko Matsuda) engage in a series of erotic encounters with the goal of experiencing every possible type of sensual pleasure. Their acts can serve as a kind of encyclopaedic summary of the sexual behaviours described in this book. In one exhibitionistic scene, Sada leads Kichi by the penis to a public alcove where they make love in full view of a washerwoman, while in another scene some geishas, who are voyeuristic witnesses to Kichi's penetration of Sada, use a dildo to pleasure themselves and then join the couple in an orgy. Sada slakes her sexual thirst by fellating Kichi, and we see

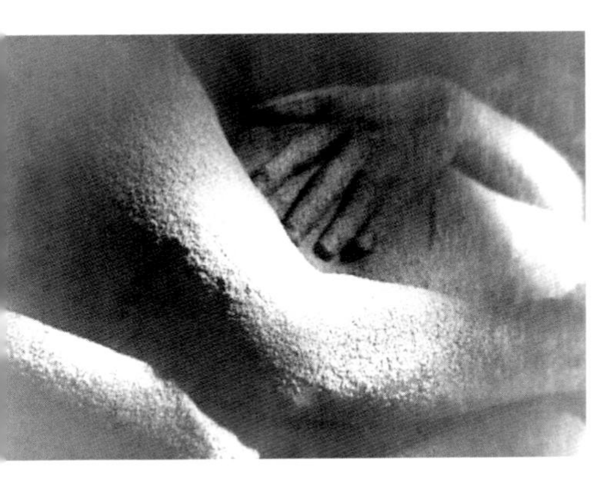

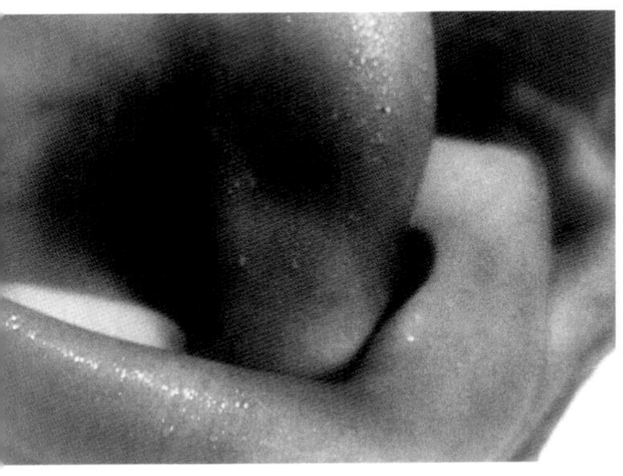

ABOVE
Stills from 'Hiroshima, mon amour' (1959)
Make love, not war: interracial limbs intertwine in this scene where a Japanese man (Eiji Okada) and a French woman (Emmanuelle Riva) have sex, while their bodies are dusted with ash fallout from the nuclear bombs that hit Hiroshima.

'Somewhere in a part of me I could not see and had not imagined, I had an opening, a cavity that was so supple and so deep that the extension of flesh that made a boy a boy, and me not one, could be accommodated there.'

Catherine Millet, *The Sexual Life of Catherine M.*

the semen running from her mouth as she raises her head from his member. Kichi uses chopsticks to season his sushi in Sada's vagina, and he is not prevented by her period from masturbating her and licking her menstrual blood from his fingers. Sada even begs Kichi to urinate inside her so that he will not have to withdraw and go use the toilet.

But the couple's desire to make love all the time, their relentless quest for the ultimate in erotic sensation, leads to ever-increasing elements of violence to ratchet up the intensity of their sex. Sada inflicts bite-wounds on Kichi. She strikes him repeatedly across the face. She threatens him with a knife and uses scissors to cut off some of his pubic hair. In the end, to sustain his erection and prolong their pleasure, she strangles him with a red scarf while she rides his sex to the ultimate orgasm – and his death. She then castrates his corpse so that she can keep him inside her, and writes on his chest in his own blood, 'Sada and Kichi, together forever.'

"I finally had an orgasm, and my doctor told me it was the wrong kind."

Tisa Farrow, *Manhattan* (1979)

BELOW
Still from 'Warm Water Under a Red Bridge' (2001)
By having sex with Misa Shimizu, Koji Yakusho risks drowning in the waters that gush from her when she climaxes.

BOTTOM
Still from 'The Ballad of Narayama' (1983)
Life for the primitive denizens of an isolated mountain village is animalistic, as in a scene where a couple has sex next to two copulating snakes.

LEFT
Still from 'In the Realm of the Senses' (1976)
As Kichi (Tatsuya Fuji) is fellated by Sada (Eiko Matsuda), geishas join them for an orgy, while a male entertainer sings of spring and winter – a reference to Sada and Kichi's May-December romance.

ABOVE
On the set of 'In the Realm of the Senses' (1976)
Director Nagisa Oshima (in the centre, wearing glasses) gives instructions to his actors in the orgy scene.

TOP
Still from 'In the Realm of the Senses' (1976)
Sada entertains Kichi while riding him. The film's varied sexual positions and colourful kimono fabrics are based on erotic woodblock prints from Japan's Edo era.

ABOVE

Still from 'In the Realm of the Senses' (1976)
Although he is legally married to another woman, Kichi takes Sada as his bride in the sexual sense. The world of physical fulfilment becomes the only meaningful one for them.

RIGHT

Still from 'In the Realm of the Senses' (1976)
After inserting a hard-boiled egg into Sada's vagina, Kichi watches while she 'lays an egg', which he will then consume as a sensual treat.

ABOVE
Still from 'In the Realm of the Senses' (1976)
Sada makes Kichi her own forever. Erotic asphyxiation (the red scarf around his neck) will become the ultimate in sexual possession (the red blood on the knife she uses to castrate him so that she can keep him always with her).

PAGES 184/185
Still from 'In the Realm of the Senses' (1976)
Sada strangles Kichi so that he will stay hard longer and extend her pleasure.

*Diane Keaton: "Do you want to perform sex?"
Woody Allen: "Perform sex? I don't think I'm up to a performance, but I'll rehearse with you, if you like."*

Sleeper (1973)

Chronology

ABOVE
On the set of 'Dr No' (1962)
Ursula Andress and Sean Connery during a break in filming this James Bond movie.

OPPOSITE TOP
On the set of 'Barbarella' (1968)
Winged angel John Phillip Law uses Jane Fonda to feather his nest in a Leda-and-the-swan moment from this popular sex comedy.

OPPOSITE BOTTOM
On the set of 'And God Created Woman' (1956)
Jean-Louis Trintignant lies with Brigitte Bardot, while director Roger Vadim arranges the sheet.

1896 A Victorian couple is the first to kiss on film in *The Kiss*. Louise Willy performs a striptease in *The Bath*.

1915 In *Daughter of the Gods*, Annette Kellerman is the first female star to appear nude on screen. *A Free Ride* is the earliest known stag (pornographic) film.

1919 *Anders als die Andern* presents male lovers at a gay ball, while *Mädchen in Uniform* (1931) depicts Sapphic attraction in a girls' boarding school, making these two films among the first to represent homosexuality and lesbianism.

1927 The irresistible *je ne sais quoi* of a nude Clara Bow makes her the "It" Girl, one of the earliest sex symbols, in *Hula*.

1930 In *Morocco*, cross-dressed in a man's tuxedo and top hat, Marlene Dietrich becomes the first leading lady to kiss another woman.

1932 A religious context is used as an excuse for eroticism in *The Sign of the Cross*, with a nude female Christian martyr tied to a post and menaced by a gorilla.

1933 *Ecstasy* becomes the first film to be blocked by US Customs from import into the country due to Hedy Lamarr's nude swimming scene and a close-up of her face during orgasm.

1934 The Motion Picture Production Code, first instituted in 1930, now begins to be enforced, partly owing to a flurry of protest over Mae West's sex comedies.

1946 Howard Hughes defies the Production Code when he exhibits Jane Russell in *The Outlaw* (1943) without a seal of approval, and the movie proves to be a smash success.

1956 *Baby Doll* – 'Condemned' by the Catholic Legion of Decency – and then *Lolita* (1962) cause a stir with their older men lusting after under-age girls.

1957 *Island in the Sun* breaches the Production Code ban on miscegenation with its two interracial romances.

1958 Brigitte Bardot introduces the bikini to America when *And God Created Woman* (1956) arrives in the US.

1959 *The Immoral Mr. Teas* inaugurates the cycle of (non-genital) nudie-cutie films, which ends when private parts are exposed in *The Raw Ones* (1966).

1960 In *Psycho*, voyeurism and a shower stabbing / implied rape mean the beginning of the end for the Production Code.

1962 *Jules and Jim* makes the *ménage à trois* a hot topic.

1965 *The Pawnbroker* becomes the first Production Code-approved film to reveal a woman's bare breasts, which are deemed integral to the story.

1966 Flashes of pubic hair make film history in *Blow-Up*. *Who's Afraid of Virginia Woolf?* deals a final blow to the Production Code with its profanity, including "hump the hostess".

1967 Sexually curious filmgoers flock to see a nude couple have (simulated) intercourse in *I Am Curious (Yellow)*. The seduction of a younger man by an older woman is risqué subject matter for a Hollywood film in *The Graduate*. In *I'll Never Forget What's'isname*, Marianne Faithfull makes movie history by being the first to say "fuck" on screen.

1968 The Production Code is replaced by a Motion Picture Association of America (MPAA) ratings system – G, M (later PG), R and X.

1969 *Midnight Cowboy* is the only X-rated film ever to win an Oscar for Best Picture. *The Damned* connects Nazism with all kinds of sexual perversions, which would be taken to an even further fascist extreme in *Salo* (1976).

1970 Raquel Welch plays a transsexual who rapes a Hollywood stud with a dildo in *Myra Breckinridge*.

1971 *Sunday, Bloody Sunday* turns heads with an extended gay kissing scene. *A Clockwork Orange* disturbs audiences with its 'Singin' in the Rain' rape sequence. *The Devils* scandalizes with its blasphemous depictions of a randy priest and erotomania among nuns.

1972 *Last Tango in Paris* is hailed by Pauline Kael as a masterpiece of erotic moviemaking, while others joke about its "go get the butter" scene of anal sex. Hardcore goes mainstream for the first time in *Deep Throat*, which ushers in a (very brief) period of 'porno chic'.

1974 The softcore *Emmanuelle* fills the gap left by the absence of hardcore films, which have now been essentially banned from mainstream theatres.

1975 Tim Curry popularizes transvestism and bisexuality in *The Rocky Horror Picture Show*.

1978 *Caligula* startles audiences with its unprecedented combination of a big-name cast and hardcore orgy scenes.

1980 Gays protest *Cruising*'s depiction of the New York S&M leather scene.

1981 *Body Heat*, with sultry femme fatale Kathleen Turner, begins a new cycle of films noirs, dubbed neo-noirs or erotic thrillers.

1984 The PG-13 rating is introduced, due in part to a sexualized torture scene in *Indiana Jones and the Temple of Doom* considered too graphic for PG but not disturbing enough for an R.

1985 In *Kiss of the Spider Woman*, William Hurt becomes the first to win a Best Actor Oscar for a homosexual role.

1990 *Henry & June* is the first major studio film to receive the new NC-17 rating.

1992 Sharon Stone exposes her sex in *Basic Instinct*. Jaye Davidson reveals that she is really a he in *The Crying Game*.

1999 American audiences are irritated by the digitally added figures that obscure the orgy scene which European viewers get to see unobstructed in *Eyes Wide Shut*.

2000 *Baise-moi*, a kind of hardcore *Thelma & Louise*, provokes a scandal when right-wing groups pressure the French government into reclassifying the film as an X and getting it banned from mainstream theatres.

2002 *Irreversible* becomes notorious for subjecting Monica Bellucci to an unbearably extended rape scene.

2003 *The Brown Bunny* causes a sensation at Cannes with its unsimulated fellatio scene.

2004 *9 Songs* presents real sex (fellatio, cunnilingus and penetration) in what has been described as the most sexually explicit film in the history of mainstream British cinema.

Filmography

Basic Instinct *(1992)*

Crew: ***Director*** Paul Verhoeven, ***Writer*** Joe Eszterhas, ***Executive Producer*** Mario Kassar, ***Producer*** Alan Marshall, ***Music*** Jerry Goldsmith, ***Cinematographer*** Jan de Bont, ***Editor*** Frank J. Urioste, ***Production Designer*** Terence Marsh, ***Special Effects*** Rob Bottin, Colour, 130 minutes.
Cast: Michael Douglas (Nick Curran), Sharon Stone (Catherine Tramell), George Dzundza (Gus Moran), Jeanne Tripplehorn (Dr. Beth Garner), Denis Arndt (Lt. Philip Walker), Leilani Sarelle (Roxy), Bruce A. Young (Andrews), Chelcie Ross (Capt. Talcott), Dorothy Malone (Hazel Dobkins), Wayne Knight (John Correli), Daniel von Bargen (Lt. Marty Nilsen), Stephen Tobolowsky (Dr. Lamott), Benjamin Mouton (Harrigan), Jack McGee (Sheriff), Bill Cable (Johnny Boz).
In *Basic Instinct* femme fatale Catherine (Sharon Stone) flaunts her body as a way of taunting Nick (Michael Douglas), the cop who suspects her of having killed a man at the climax of S&M sex.

Betty Blue

(37°2 le matin, 1986)
Crew: ***Director & Writer*** Jean-Jacques Beineix, ***Novel*** Philippe Djian, ***Producers*** Jean-Jacques Beineix, Claudie Ossard, ***Music*** Gabriel Yared, ***Cinematographer*** Jean-François Robin, ***Editors*** Marie-Aimée Debril, Monique Prim, ***Production Designer*** Carlos Conti, Colour, 120 minutes (director's cut 185 minutes).
Cast: Jean-Hugues Anglade (Zorg), Béatrice Dalle (Betty), Gérard Darmon (Eddy), Consuelo De Haviland (Lisa), Clémentine Célarié (Annie), Jacques Mathou (Bob), Richard (Vincent Lindon).
In *Betty Blue*, Betty's uninhibited lust does not drain her lover Zorg, but inspires his passion and creativity.

Crash *(1996)*

Crew: ***Director & Writer*** David Cronenberg, ***Novel*** J.G. Ballard, ***Executive Producers*** Robert Lantos, Jeremy Thomas, ***Co-Executive Producers*** Chris Auty, Andras Hamori, ***Producer*** David Cronenberg, ***Music*** Howard Shore, ***Cinematographer*** Peter Suschitzky, ***Editor*** Ronald Sanders, ***Production Designer*** Carol Spier, Colour, 100 minutes.
Cast: James Spader (James Ballard), Holly Hunter (Helen Remington), Elias Koteas (Vaughan), Deborah Kara Unger (Catherine Ballard), Rosanna Arquette (Gabrielle), Peter MacNeill (Colin Seagrave), Yolande Julian (Airport Hooker), Cheryl Swarts (Vera Seagrave), David Cronenberg (Voice of Auto Wreck Salesman).
Crash focuses on a subculture of auto-accident survivors who have become sexually obsessed with witnessing and re-enacting car crashes.

In the Realm of the Senses

(Ai No Corrida, 1976)
Crew: ***Director & Writer*** Nagisa Oshima, ***Executive Producer*** Koji Wakamatsu, ***Producer*** Anatole Dauman, ***Music*** Minoru Miki, ***Cinematographer*** Hideo Itoh, ***Editors*** Patrick Sauvion, Keiichi Uraoka, ***Production Designer*** Jusho Toda, Colour, 105 minutes.
Cast: Tatsuya Fuji (Kichi Ishida), Eiko Matsuda (Sada Abe), Aoi Nakajima (Toku), Yasuko Matsui (Tagawa Inn Manager), Meika Seri (Matsuko – Yoshidaya Maid), Kanae Kobayashi (Old Geisha Kikuryu), Taiji Tonoyama (Old Beggar), Kyôji Kokonoe (Teacher Omiya), Naomi Shiraishi (Geisha Yaeji), Shinkichi Noda (Old Restaurant Man).
In the Realm of the Senses shows inn owner Kichi and his maid-turned-lover Sada engage in a series of erotic encounters with the goal of experiencing every possible type of sensual pleasure.

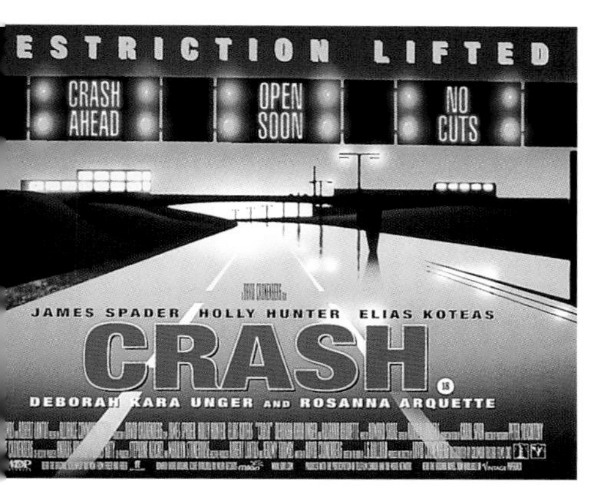

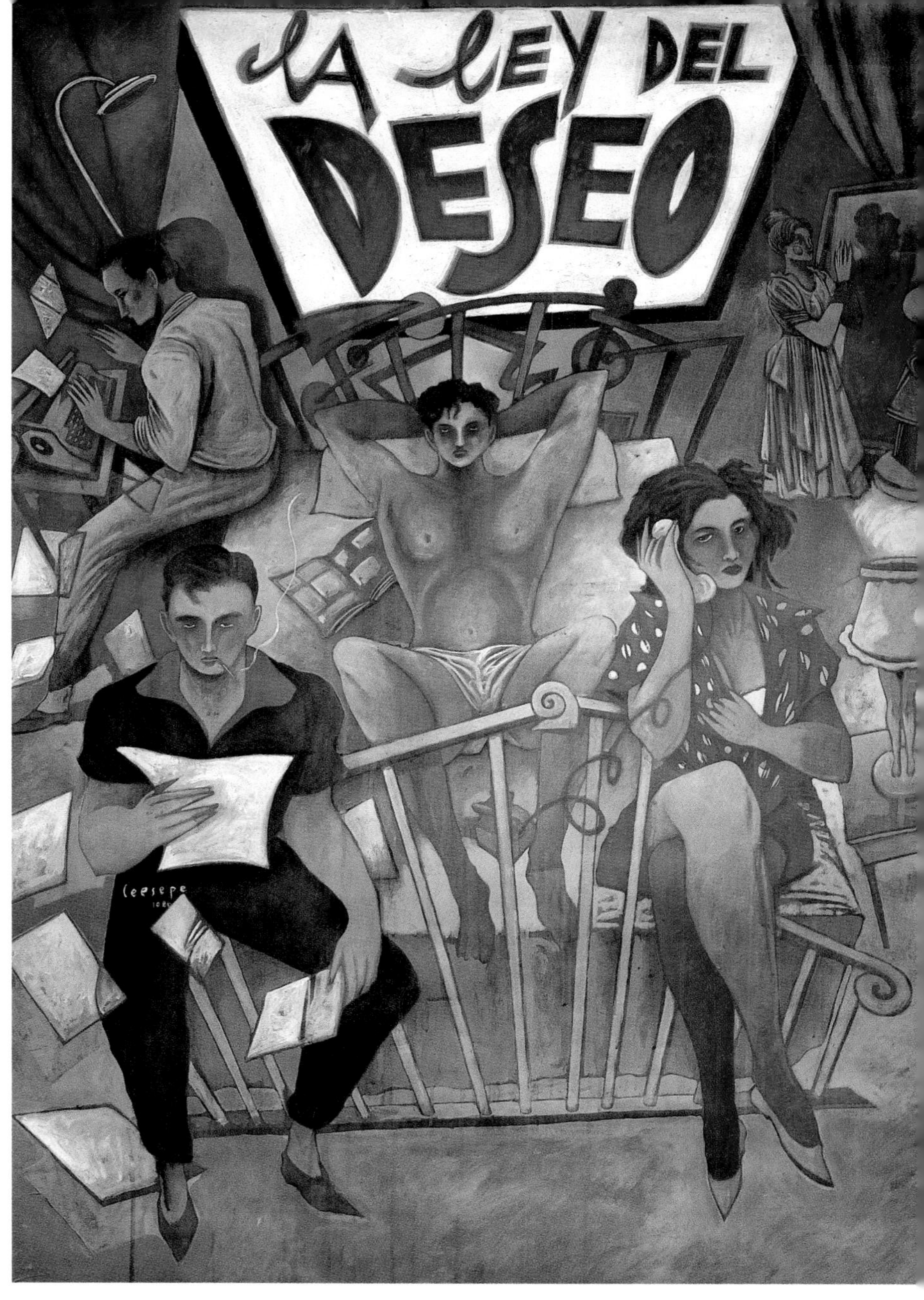

Kids *(1995)*

Crew: ***Director*** Larry Clark, ***Writer*** Harmony Korine, ***Story*** Larry Clark, Jim Lewis, ***Executive Producers*** Michael Chambers, Patrick Panzarella, Gus Van Sant, ***Producer*** Cary Woods, ***Music*** Lou Barlow, John Davis, ***Cinematographer*** Eric Alan Edwards, ***Editor*** Christopher Tellesfen, ***Production Designer*** Kevin Thompson, Colour, 91 minutes.

Cast: Leo Fitzpatrick (Telly), Justin Pierce (Casper), Chloë Sevigny (Jennie), Yakira Peguero (Darcy), Rosario Dawson (Ruby), Sarah Henderson (Girl #1), Joseph Chan (Deli Owner), Johnathan Staci Kim (Korean Guy), Adriane Brown (Little Girl), Sajan Bhagat (Paul), Billy Valdes (Stanley), Billy Waldeman (Zack), Javier Nunez (Javier), Luis Nunez (Luis), Christian Bruna (Christian), Alex Glen (Alex).

Kids follows Jennie, who contracted the HIV virus when she lost her virginity to Telly, in her quest to find him before he infects another girl.

Last Tango in Paris *(1972)*

Crew: ***Director*** Bernardo Bertolucci, ***Writers*** Bernardo Bertolucci, Franco Arcalli, ***Additional Dialogue*** Agnès Varda, ***Producer*** Alberto Grimaldi, ***Music*** Gato Barbieri, ***Cinematographer*** Vittorio Storaro, ***Editors*** Franco Arcalli, Roberto Perpignani, ***Production Designer*** Ferdinando Scarfiotti, Colour, 136 minutes.

Cast: Marlon Brando (Paul), Maria Schneider (Jeanne), Jean-Pierre Léaud (Tom), Maria Michi (Rosa's Mother), Giovanna Galletti (Prostitute), Gitt Magrini (Jeanne's Mother), Catherine Allégret (Catherine), Luce Marquand (Olympia), Marie-Hélène Breillat (Monique), Catherine Breillat (Mouchette).

In *Last Tango in Paris* Paul and Jeanne, who know nothing about each other, not even their names, meet daily in an empty Paris apartment for pure uncomplicated sex.

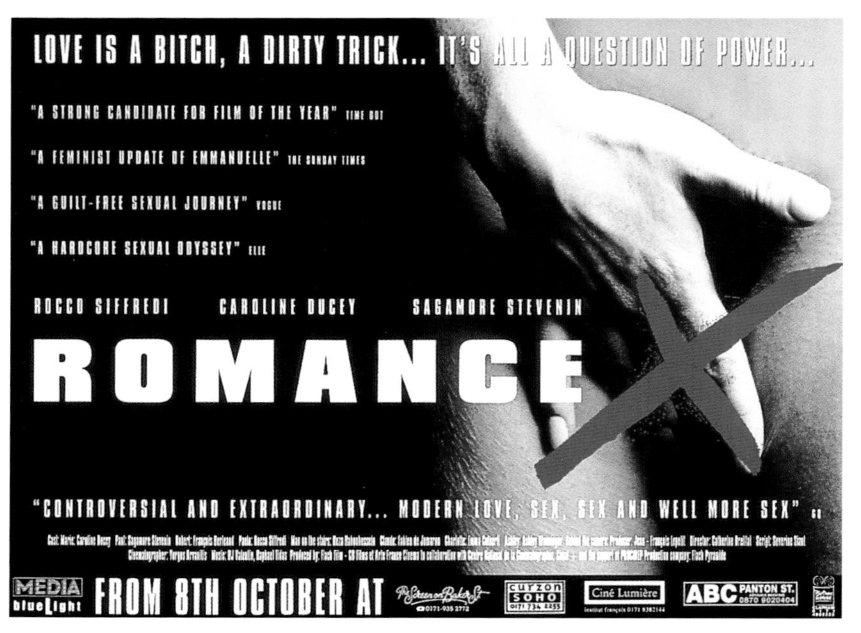

Romance *(1999)*

Crew: ***Director & Writer*** Catherine Breillat, ***Executive Producer*** Catherine Jacques, ***Producer*** Jean-François Lepetit, ***Music*** Raphaël Tidas, D.J. Valentin, ***Cinematographer*** Yorgos Arvanitis, ***Editor*** Agnès Guillemot, ***Production Designer*** Frédérique Belvaux, Colour, 99 minutes.
Cast: Caroline Ducey (Marie), Sagamore Stévenin (Paul), François Berléand (Robert), Rocco Siffredi (Paolo), Reza Habouhossein (Man on Stairs), Ashley Wanninger (Ashley), Emma Colberti (Charlotte), Fabien de Jomaron (Claude).
In *Romance*, teacher Marie is emotionally involved with her boyfriend Paul but his lack of interest in sex leads her to find sexual fulfilment elsewhere.

Law of Desire
(La Ley del Deseo, 1987)

Crew: ***Director & Writer*** Pedro Almodóvar, ***Executive Producer*** Miguel Angel Pérez Campos, ***Associate Producer*** Agustín Almodóvar, ***Music*** Bernardo Bonezzi, ***Cinematographer*** Angel Luis Fernández, ***Editor*** José Salcedo, ***Art Director*** Javier Fernández, Colour, 102 minutes.
Cast: Eusebio Poncela (Pablo Quintero), Carmen Maura (Tina Quintero), Antonio Banderas (Antonio Benítez), Miguel Molina (Juan Bermúdez), Fernando Guillén (Inspector de policía), Manuela Velasco (Ada, niña), Nacho Martínez (Doctor Martin), Bibí Andersen (Ada), Helga Liné (Madre Antonio), Germán Cobos (El Cura).
Law of Desire challenges audiences with the complexity of its gay and trans-gendered characters.

The Night Porter
(Il Portiere di Notte, 1974)

Crew: ***Director*** Liliana Cavani, ***Writers*** Liliana Cavani, Italo Moscati, ***Producers*** Esa De Simone, Robert Gordon Edwards, ***Music*** Daniele Paris, ***Cinematographer*** Alfio Contini, ***Editor*** Franco Arcalli, ***Art Directors*** Nedo Azzini, Jean Marie Simon, Colour, 122 minutes.
Cast: Dirk Bogarde (Maximilian Theo Aldorfer), Charlotte Rampling (Lucia Atherton), Philippe Leroy (Klaus), Gabriele Ferzetti (Hans), Giuseppe Addobbati (Stumm), Isa Miranda (Countess Stein), Nino Bignamini (Adolph), Marino Masé (Atherton), Amedeo Amodio (Bert).
In *The Night Porter*, Max, a former SS officer, is working nights as a hotel porter in Vienna, when he meets Lucia, a former concentration camp inmate, and the two of them begin to re-enact the master/slave relationship they had in the camp.

Y tu mamá también *(2001)*

Crew: ***Director*** Alfonso Cuarón, ***Writers*** Alfonso Cuarón, Carlos Cuarón, ***Executive Producers*** Sergio Aguero, Amy Kaufman, David Linde, ***Producers*** Alfonso Cuarón, Jorge Vergara, ***Music*** Natalie Imbruglia, Frank Zappa, ***Cinematographer*** Emmanuel Lubezki, ***Editors*** Alfonso Cuarón, Alex Rodríguez, ***Production Designers*** Marc Bedia, Miguel Angel Alvarez, Colour, 105 minutes.
Cast: Diego Luna (Tenoch Iturbide), Gael García Bernal (Julio Zapata), Maribel Verdú (Luisa Cortés), Ana López Mercado (Ana Morelos), Nathan Grinberg (Manuel Huerta), Verónica Langer (María Eugenia Calles de Huerta), María Aura (Cecilia Huerta), Giselle Audirac (Nicole Bazaine), Arturo Ríos (Esteban Morelos), Andrés Almeida (Diego "Saba" Madero), Diana Bracho (Silivia Allende de Iturbide), Emilio Echevarria (Miguel Iturbide), Marta Aura (Enriqueta "Queta" Allende), Juan Carlos Remolina (Alejandro "Jano" Montes de Oca).
Y Tu Mamá También follows two horny Mexican teens as they try to score with a gorgeous Spanish woman whilst accompanying her on a beach vacation.

Acknowledgements

It is my pleasure to thank Paul Duncan for his excellent advice during the planning stages of this book, his tenacity in tracking down erotic images from so many movies, and his expert, tactful and inspiring input as editor. I would also like to thank all my colleagues at Cal Poly who suggested movie scenes that have excited them in their years as filmgoers, and I ask them to forgive me for not being able to include every one of their titillating tips. I am grateful to Katie Tool for her absolutely indispensable clerical and emotional support, and to the Interlibrary Loan staff at the Kennedy Library – Linda Hauck, Michael Price, and Janice Stone – for going the extra distance in helping me to obtain vital research materials in a timely fashion. Finally, I would like to thank my wife, Helen Bailey, who has been by turns muse, critic, provocateur and helpmate. She is my one true love.

Bibliography

Erotic Cinema

- **Anger, Kenneth:** *Hollywood Babylon.* Dell 1975
- **Atkins, Thomas R. (ed.):** *Sexuality in the Movies.* Da Capo 1975
- **Bell-Metereau, Rebecca:** *Hollywood Androgyny.* Columbia University Press 1993
- **Bernard, Jami:** *Total Exposure: The Movie Buff's Guide to Celebrity Nude Scenes.* Citadel Press 1999
- **Bouzereau, Laurent:** *The Cutting Room Floor.* Citadel Press 1994
- **Briggs, Joe Bob:** *Profoundly Disturbing: Shocking Movies That Changed History!* Universe 2003
- **Brode, Douglas:** *Sinema: Erotic Adventures in Film.* Citadel Press 2002
- **Doherty, Thomas:** *Pre-Code Hollywood: Sex, Immorality, and Insurrection in American Cinema, 1930-1934.* Columbia University Press 1999
- **Dyer, Richard & Pidduck, Julianne:** *Now You See It: Studies on Lesbian and Gay Film.* Routledge 2002
- **Eberwein, Robert:** *Sex Ed: Film, Video, and the Framework of Desire.* Rutgers University Press 1999
- **Farber, Stephen:** *The Movie Rating Game.* Public Affairs Press 1972
- **Fentone, Steve:** *AntiCristo: The Bible of Nasty Nun Sinema and Culture.* FAB Press 2000
- **Flint, David:** *Babylon Blue.* Creation Books 1999
- **Frank, Sam:** *Sex in the Movies.* Citadel Press 1986
- **Fulwood, Neil:** *One Hundred Sex Scenes That Changed Cinema.* Batsford 2003
- **Gardner, Gerald:** *The Censorship Papers: Movie Censorship Letters from the Hays Office, 1934 to 1968.* Dodd, Mead 1987
- **Haskell, Molly:** *From Reverence to Rape: The Treatment of Women in the Movies.* Penguin 1974
- **Hosoda, Craig:** *The Bare Facts Video Guide 1996: Where to Find Your Favorite Actors & Actresses Nude on Videotape.* Bare Facts 1995
- **Hunter, Jack:** *Eros in Hell: Sex, Blood and Madness in Japanese Cinema.* Creation Books 1998
- **Jouffa, François & Crawley, Tony:** *L'Age d'Or du Cinéma Erotique et Pornographique, 1973-1976.* Ramsay 2003
- **Kabir, Shameem:** *Daughters of Desire: Lesbian Representations in Film.* Cassell 1998
- **Lang, Robert:** *Masculine Interests: Homoerotics in Hollywood Film.* Columbia University Press 2002
- **LaSalle, Mick:** *Complicated Women: Sex and Power in Pre-Code Hollywood.* St. Martin's Press 2000
- **LaSalle, Mick:** *Dangerous Men: Pre-Code Hollywood and the Birth of the Modern Man.* St. Martin's Press 2002
- **Lehman, Peter:** *Running Scared: Masculinity and the Representation of the Male Body.* Temple University Press 1993
- **Lenne, Gérard:** *Erotisme et Cinéma.* La Musardine 1998
- **Lenne, Gérard:** *Sex on the Screen: Eroticism in Film.* St. Martin's Press 1985
- **Lenne, Gérard:** *Sex on the Screen: The Eighties.* St. Martin's Press 1990
- **Lewis, Jon:** *Hollywood v. Hard Core: How the Struggle Over Censorship Saved the Modern Film Industry.* New York University Press 2000
- **Lort, Don:** *Coming of Age: Movie and Video Guide.* Companion Press 1997
- **Lyons, Charles:** *The New Censors: Movies and the Culture Wars.* Temple University Press 1997
- **Mathijs, Ernest & Mendik, Xavier (eds.):** *Alternative Europe: Eurotrash and Exploitation Cinema Since 1945.* Wallflower Press 2004
- **McCarthy, Helen & Clements, Jonathan:** *The Erotic Anime Movie Guide.* Overlook Press 1999
- **McDonagh, Maitland:** *The 50 Most Erotic Films of All Time.* Citadel Press 1996
- **Miller, Frank:** *Censored Hollywood: Sex, Sin, & Violence on Screen.* Turner Publishing 1994
- **Muller, Eddie & Faris, Daniel:** *Grindhouse: The Forbidden World of "Adults Only" Cinema.* St. Martin's Griffin 1996
- **Olson, Jenni:** *The Queer Movie Poster Book.* Chronicle Books 2004
- **Pascall, Jeremy & Jeavons, Clyde:** *A Pictorial History of Sex in the Movies.* Hamlyn 1975
- **Philips, Baxter:** *Cut: The Unseen Cinema.* Bounty Books 1975
- **Radney, Hilary and Luckett, Moya (eds.):** *Swinging Single: Representing Sexuality in the 1960s.* University of Minnesota Press 1999
- **Rondeau, Xavier:** *L'Enfant-Femme à l'Ecran: Le Cinéma des Fillettes Séductrices.* Dreamland 2003
- **Rotsler, William:** *Contemporary Erotic Cinema.* Ballantine Books 1973
- **Russo, Vito:** *The Celluloid Closet: Homosexuality in the Movies.* Harper & Row 1987
- **Schaefer, Eric:** *"Bold! Daring! Shocking! True!": A History of Exploitation Films, 1919-1959.* Duke University Press 1999
- **Shipman, David:** *Caught in the Act: Sex and Eroticism in the Movies.* Elm Tree Books 1985
- **Sinclair, Marianne:** *Hollywood Lolitas: The Nymphet Syndrome in the Movies.* Henry Holt 1988
- **Sova, Dawn B.:** *Forbidden Films: Censorship Histories of 125 Motion Pictures.* Checkmark Books 2001
- **Springer, Claudia:** *Electronic Eros: Bodies and Desire in the Postindustrial Age.* University of Texas Press 1996
- **Stevenson, Jack (ed.):** *Fleshpot: Cinema's Sexual Myth Makers & Taboo Breakers.* Headpress 2000
- **Stewart, Steve (ed.):** *Campy, Vampy, Trampy Movie Quotes: 910 Bitchy Barbs, Wicked Wisecracks & Lusty Lampoons.* Companion Press 1996
- **Stewart, Steve:** *Full Frontal: Male Nudity Video Guide.* Companion Press 1996
- **Straayer, Chris:** *Deviant Eyes, Deviant Bodies: Sexual Re-Orientation in Film and Video.* Columbia University Press 1996
- **Studlar, Gaylyn:** *In the Realm of Pleasure: Von Sternberg, Dietrich, and the Masochistic Aesthetic.* University of Illinois Press 1988
- **Studlar, Gaylyn:** *This Mad Masquerade: Stardom and Masculinity in the Jazz Age.* Columbia University Press 1996
- **Tohill, Cathal & Tombs, Pete:** *Immoral Tales: European Sex and Horror Movies, 1956-1984.* St. Martin's Griffin 1995
- **Tyler, Parker:** *A Pictorial History of Sex in Films.* Citadel Press 1974
- **Tyler, Parker:** *Screening the Sexes: Homosexuality in the Movies.* Da Capo Press 1993
- **Vieira, Mark A.:** *Sin in Soft Focus: Pre-Code Hollywood.* Harry N. Abrams 1999
- **Walker, Alexander:** *Sex in the Movies.* Pelican 1968
- **Waugh, Thomas:** *Hard to Imagine: Gay Male Eroticism in Photography and Film from Their Beginnings to Stonewall.* Columbia University Press 1996
- **Weiss, Andrea:** *Vampires & Violets: Lesbians in Film.* Penguin 1993
- **White, Patricia:** *Uninvited: Classical Hollywood Cinema and Lesbian Representability.* Indiana University Press 1999
- **Williams, Linda:** *Hard Core: Power, Pleasure, and the "Frenzy of the Visible."* University of California Press 1999
- **Wortley, Richard:** *Erotic Movies.* Crescent Books 1975

Sexual Behaviour and Erogenous Zones

- **Bader, Michael J.:** *Arousal: The Secret Logic of Sexual Fantasies.* St. Martin's Press 2002
- **Bataille, Georges:** *Erotism: Death & Sensuality.* City Lights Books 1986
- **Blackledge, Catherine:** *The Story of V: A Natural History of Female Sexuality.* Rutgers University Press 2004
- **Blue, Adrianne:** *On Kissing: Travels in an Intimate Landscape.* Kodansha 1997
- **Dally, Peter:** *The Fantasy Game: How Male and Female Sexual Fantasies Affect Our Lives.* Stein and Day 1975
- **Drenth, Jelto:** *The Origin of the World: A History of the Vagina.* Consortium 2004
- **Fanon, Frantz:** *Black Skin, White Masks.* Paladin 1970
- **Foucault, Michel:** *The History of Sexuality.* Pantheon Books 1978
- **Friday, Nancy:** *Men in Love: Men's Sexual Fantasies: The Triumph of Love Over Rage.* Delacorte 1980
- **Friedman, David M.:** *A Mind of Its Own: A Cultural History of the Penis.* Free Press 2001
- **Garber, Marjorie:** *Dog Love.* Simon & Schuster 1996
- **Garber, Marjorie:** *Vested Interests: Cross-Dressing and Cultural Anxiety.* Routledge 1992
- **Garber, Marjorie:** *Vice Versa: Bisexuality and the Eroticism of Everyday Life.* Simon & Schuster 1995
- **Groneman, Carol:** *Nymphomania: A History.* Norton 2000
- **Hall, Donald E. & Pramaggiore, Maria (ed.):** *RePresenting Bisexualities: Subjects and Cultures of Fluid Desire.* New York University Press 1996
- **Hamilton, Terri:** *Skin Flutes & Velvet Gloves: A Collection of Facts and Fancies, Legends and Oddities about the Body's Private Parts.* St. Martin's Press 2003
- **Kennedy, Randall:** *Interracial Intimacies: Sex, Marriage, Identity, and Adoption.* Pantheon Books 2003
- **Kipnis, Laura:** *Bound and Gagged: Pornography and the Politics of Fantasy in America.* Grove Press 1996
- **Laqueur, Thomas W.:** *Solitary Sex: A Cultural History of Masturbation.* Zone Books 2003
- **Levine, Judith:** *Harmful to Minors: The Perils of Protecting Children from Sex.* University of Minnesota Press 2002
- **Margolis, Jonathan:** *O: The Intimate History of the Orgasm.* Grove Press 2004
- **McClintock, Anne:** 'Maid to Order: Commercial S/M and Gender Power' in **Pamela Church Gibson (ed.):** *More Dirty Looks: Gender, Pornography and Power.* British Film Institute 2004, pgs. 237-53
- **Millet, Catherine:** *The Sexual Life of Catherine M.* Grove Press 2002
- **Petersen, James R.:** *The Century of Sex: Playboy's History of the Sexual Revolution: 1900-1999.* Grove Press 1999
- **Réage, Pauline:** *Story of O.* Grove Press 1965
- **Segal, Lynne:** 'Only the Literal: The Contradictions of Anti-Pornography Feminism' in **Pamela Church Gibson (ed.):** *More Dirty Looks: Gender, Pornography and Power.* British Film Institute 2004, pgs. 59-70
- **Soble, Alan:** *Pornography, Sex, and Feminism.* Prometheus 2002
- **Sontag, Susan:** 'Fascinating Fascism' in *Under the Sign of Saturn.* Vintage Books 1981, pgs. 73-105
- **Sontag, Susan:** 'The Pornographic Imagination' in *Styles of Radical Will.* Dell 1970, pgs. 35-73
- **Steele, Valerie:** *The Corset: A Cultural History.* Yale University Press 2001
- **Thurman, Judith:** 'Altered States' in *The New Yorker.* 17 December 2001, pgs. 93-96
- **Turner, E.S.:** *A History of Courting.* Dutton 1955
- **Yalom, Marilyn:** *A History of the Breast.* Ballantine Books 1998

PAGE 192

Still from 'Era Lui... Si! Si!' (1951)

Luscious Sophia Loren as a bare-breasted extra in one of her earliest films. Noel Coward once said about Sophia Loren that "She should have been sculpted in chocolate truffles so that the world could devour her."